A PRACTICAL GUIDE TO GENERATING SALES LEADS FOR MARKETING MANAGERS, SALES LEADERS, OWNERS & OPERATORS OF B2B COMPANIES.

By: John Buie & Jason Hagerman

Published By: Journey Better Business Group Inc.

FOREWORD

John Buie   **Jason Hagerman**

We wrote this book because there's an epidemic of imposter syndrome in marketing and sales professionals working in business to business (B2B). It was there when we started in B2B 20+ years ago and it's here today. We felt it at the beginning. And the feeling took years to overcome.

You know what it's like.

- I'm not a chemist. How can I speak to our lab customers with any authority?

- I can't even assemble my Ikea bookshelf without the instructions. How can I communicate the value of these sawmills to the pulp and paper industry?

- The last time I tried to operate a skidsteer I was 17, and I almost flipped it. Who's going to buy one from me when all I can tell them is they won't flip over?

- I pay someone to change my car's tires. I'll never be able to convince Bridgestone our company's rubber is going to make their molds more durable.

After a lot of trial and error. A lot marketing books and podcasts. A lot of long nights looking at data. A lot of detailed analyses of competing brands. It became clear that **everybody thinks everybody else knows more.**

With that revelation, we were freed from our own imposter syndromes. And we built a process that seemed logical and thorough for ourselves. We used it (still do). And it worked (still does).

And even though your business is unique, your challenges aren't entirely. **Getting sales leads is a heck of an ongoing challenge** every B2B faces.

Today, imposters unite!

This book will help you overcome your imposter syndrome and **teach you how to generate more sales leads** with a straightforward evergreen sales-lead-generating-strategy.

> The evergreen element of this strategy is important because most B2Bs exist on a hamster wheel. Create marketing campaign. Send it. Create another. It's a world of one-offs. A stressful, low-return world to live in.

You'll come out of this with more valuable, practical knowledge than the people in your industry who look confident, but should actually be frozen solid by <u>their</u> imposter syndrome.

Bill at company XYZ might look like he knows what he's doing. But **you will honestly know what you're doing.**

Now, if you already beat this imposter syndrome and you're hiring or managing newbies in the business, we're going to give you some rocket fuel.

With this book in your hands, you'll be able to generate more inbound sales leads yourself, generate more with in-house resources, or direct and audit your 3rd party agencies better.

Your power will be increased 100X.

By reading this book and doing the things in these pages, you're doing more than almost every business in your space.

Here's something else.

This is a choose your own adventure book. Go where you want or need to go. The copy you hold in your hands is yours. Obviously. But we want you to be free of the social conventions of book reading!

Skip chapters. Come back to them or don't.

Read only the sections that relate to you, whether you are the one doing the marketing work, or creating the strategy, or doing this as part of 15 other roles you occupy in the company. This book is presented with streams for each of you, with the exact steps you can follow based on your role, your skills, the things you spend your time doing now, and the time you can commit to generating new, valuable sales leads.

These streams include the three C's. Claire the Creator, Charles the Conductor, and Chris the Curator. **Which one are you?**

Claire the Creator works on the day-to-day creation of lead generating materials. He or she is a digital marketer with 1-6 years of experience. Or the digital marketing manager at a small company with no direct reports creating assets.

Charles the Conductor is in charge of others. If you're Charles, you're the boss. You're further in your career than most. You own the business or you manage others in the business. You have more experience and more responsibilities. And you need to manage your creators confidently.

Chris the Curator is involved in generating leads as a secondary, or thirdondary, or further tertiary part of the job. You're the sales manager or operations manager with lots of responsibilities, few resources, and slivers of time to dedicate to generating more leads. But it has to be done.

So you can stick to the section that relates most closely to your day-to-day experience. Or you can read every page slowly and carefully. Highlight words. Keep sticky notes nearby. Whatever you want to squeeze every bit of value from these pages.

Or use only the checklists and resources you find throughout the book.

It's all yours. And we, the authors, ask this one thing of you.

Act on what you learn in here. Grow your business. Glean affection from your boss. Rise quickly in your career. Do cool work and tell your family about it.

Follow the journey that inspires you in the pages you hold, then **stop reading and go do it.**

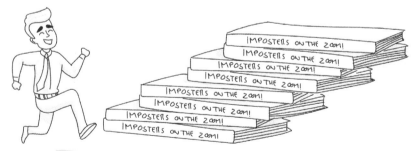

We wrote this book now to help B2Bs grow in challenging times: shipping costs are volatile, product shortages are regular, tradeshows aren't what they were, raw material expenses are explosive, AI is changing how everyone works, good staff are harder to find…you know it all.

The point is, the roadmap you used to achieve success in the past is in tatters. **Your new roadmap has that fresh book smell in your hands.**

And what good would a map be without a peppering of hidden treasures? A keen eye will read this and learn important lessons about:

1. Overcoming imposter syndrome by overcoming your ideas about uniqueness.

2. Communicating with developers and designers.

3. Using AI to build remarkably deep buyer personas.

4. Selling to and working with Creators, Curators, and Conductors.

5. Doing more with fewer staff.

6. Finding creative, engaging, and unique angles to speak to the humans behind B2B - something more like B2BE (the business to business end user)

7. Training and developing staff with less effort, a gentle learning curve, and awesome outcomes.

8. Why evergreen is the key B2B.

9. Focusing your energy on selling more products that are behavior changing.

10. Finding and winning specific windows of opportunity when your prospect is in an elevated buying mindset.

11. Leaning on your brand story to motivate GenZ and attract talent.

12. The mistakes brands from budding to behemoth make, and positioning yours smarter.

Each of these treasures is a deep conversation on its own. Worth your time and attention (and if you want to continue any of these conversations with us, email **friends@jbbgi.com** - we love talking about these things with new friends in our community).

This book is your continuing education. We update it every year. We constantly test new, simple strategies at scale, validating quickly whether they're worth following more deeply or not.

And if they're worth it, they're added to next year's release.

In these pages we aren't talking about Zappos, Tesla, Apple, Dollar Shave Club, or some other behemoth.

This is about the business you're running. Or trying to run. Or building your career in. From two employees to 200. Growing manageably. Adding profits without adding costs.

"Sales leads" are like weight loss for B2Bs. There's a ton of bad advice out there. Lots that'll tank your business. Lots that's not practical. Scroll down your feed on whatever social media platform you prefer. See the thread that says:

- *5 minutes reading this will get you more sales leads than anything else you do this month.*

Or

- *These three tricks help me capture 100 sales leads every week, and you can start using them today for free.*

If it was that easy…

But nobody gives away their secrets for free (and that's why this book wasn't free).

You already invested in this book. You gave us your trust. So you can have our secrets. If you read this cover to cover, it will be the most valuable 180 minutes you spend with your feet up this year.

Why listen to us instead of the influencers?

1. Everything you've read in the last 5 minutes resonates with you.

2. We're practitioners in the same seat as you, and we generated more than 36,000 sales leads for our B2B manufacturers and distributors in 2022.

3. That's our 10th straight year doing it.

We poured our experience into this book for two additional reasons (other than the imposter syndrome issue).

- To make money.
- To help you make money.

We wrote this to 10X your success alongside our own. And we don't succeed if you don't. So you better believe it's going to help you.

And when it does, tell us about it. We want to hear about your journey. Your success. Your growth.

Your happiness.

Because **when you're successful at work,** you carry the byproducts of that success home. You're less stressed. You're comfortable. **You're present with your family. You're living the way you want.**

Creators, Conductors, and Curators each have a path to take on the B2B Revenue Growth Journey. We're glad you decided to embark on yours today.

TABLE OF CONTENTS

Chapter 1 1
Within 6 months you're going to be more successful.

Chapter 2 10
Learn the truths your B2B competitors ignore.

Chapter 3 18
Step # 1. Develop better USPs than brands 20X your size.

Chapter 4 26
Step # 2. Create something your prospects can't live without.

Chapter 5 40
Establish yourself as the industry visionary.

Chapter 6 63
Instantly inspire confidence and trust in your prospects.

Chapter 7 73
Save your prospects time and energy to win the sale.

Chapter 8 88
Step # 3. Easily convince your prospects to share their contact info.

Chapter 9 106
Step # 4. Increase the value of every marketing asset you or your staff create.

Chapter 10 108
Bring a ton more organic prospects to your website for the next 5 years.

TABLE OF CONTENTS

Chapter 11 113
Explode the lifetime value of every customer.

Chapter 12 135
Put every new prospect at ease for the next 6 months with 30
minutes of work.

Chapter 13 140
Use YouTube to make your job easier.

Chapter 14 148
Stop freaking out about social media.

Chapter 15 153
Step # 5. 10X the effect of everything you did in the last 12 chapters.

Chapter 16 186
Overcome your greatest fears with paid ads.

Chapter 17 204
Step # 6. Make sure customers and prospects never forget your brand
+ buy from you twice as often.

Chapter 18 220
Enjoy the fruits of your labor.

Appendix A: **Services** . . . . A
Appendix B: **Acknowledgments** . . . . B

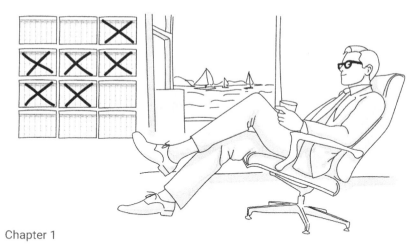

Chapter 1

WITHIN 6 MONTHS YOU'RE GOING TO BE MORE SUCCESSFUL.

This book is for people who want to make more money. People who want to grow a business. People who want to progress in their careers. People who want accountability for the employees and colleagues around them.

Maybe most importantly, people who want to come home to their families without the stress of the job in tow.

This will help you feel confident in the work you do, and comfortable knowing you do it well.

As you read in the foreword (and if you skipped it, shame on you! It's really good), this book is full of valuable insights and strategies for everyone in your organization who cares about increasing sales leads and revenue.

But we don't want anyone to waste time sifting through material that isn't for them. So we separated everything we could into streams. Three of them. Which we call The Three C's.

- Claire the Creator (content marketer, marketing manager without staff)
- Charles the Conductor (director, VP, C-suite, owner)
- Chris the Curator (sales manager, operations manager)

If you want the short descriptions of each of these, flip quickly back to page iii. And if you want to get really hyped about what this book is going to help you do - and help you become - read on.

For the in-the-trenches marketing person - **Claire the Creator**

If you're a skimmer of books and all you really want is to learn **how to** - starting out as an intern or looking for fresh ideas as an experienced marketer - **get more sales leads**, here you go!

The size of the business doesn't matter.

You could be the only marketing person at a 40-year-old small business with 9 staff and a cat. Or the newest member of a marketing squad in a publicly traded enterprise with thousands of employees and casual Fridays and too many meetings.

If work for a business selling to other businesses and your responsibility is to create marketing materials in one way or another for this business, **you're going to get really good at it really fast.** You'll be on marketing steroids, without any of the nasty side effects.

Everything in these chapters can be implemented to drive your growth. Personal, career, and the growth you're responsible for driving in the business tomorrow.

Do what you want with it.

You could pick 60-80% of the deliverables we outline and generate results.

BUT!

All these deliverables act as force multipliers.

Do a little more, get a ton more results.

So if you're serious about growth. Growth in your role. In your career. Growth of the business. You're holding the roadmap.

Here's what will happen when you use these strategies in your marketing program over the next year.

1.   Your colleagues will notice signs of the business improving.

2.   Your manager will see the impact of *your new* direction.

3.   You'll get more recognition from the leaders in the business.

4.   You'll become an integral part of the business, and you'll find yourself invited to discussions that center around driving the growth of the business you're employed by.

Maybe you're frustrated you're not invited to those discussions right now.

Unless they worked in marketing themselves, senior management/executives often look at marketing as an arms length tactical role. The first marketing hires they ever made where photoshop and illustrator technicians they brought on to build catalogs. When digital became the thing to do, those technicians became the website builders and digital marketing "experts" on the team. It's why you still see job ads for marketers to do everything. Graphic design, write content, manage social media, manage website updates, perform market research, and more.

But that view is changing. Rightly. And if you want to be part of the high level discussions in the business, **you have to be awesome at driving sales leads.** And you have to be able to prove your awesomeness with data.

Oh right. We forgot the parts you really care about

1. You'll get a bigger salary.

2. You'll get a bigger team to manage.

3. You'll get a bigger budget.

4. You'll have more creative freedom.

5. You'll have job security (or ammunition to use in your job hunt).

6. You'll have freedom and trust from your manager, so they're not constantly questioning you or looking over your shoulder.

As you feather through this book, you'll see three different tracks of information. Different journeys for different professionals. You've seen it above already. Claire the Creator, Charles the Conductor, Chris the Curator.

You walk the path of Claire the Creator.

There are tips or tricks that are only applicable to someone with your technical and creative physiology.

If you want to understand other angles on the business you work in, you'll find those on Charles the Conductor and Chris the Curator's paths.

The Second C, Charles the Conductor - For the marketing director, business owner, or business operator

<u>You're Charles the Conductor.</u>

A business owner or operator with a refined sense of your business' core competencies. Or a marketing director with a heap of experience and the maturity to be invested in the success of your business beyond your regular paycheck. You lead others in the business, and their success directly contributes to your own.

If you're the owner/operator, you keep your customers happy, but you don't love digging for new leads. You probably just ignore it. Because the business is stable and reliable. Things are fine.

But it wouldn't take a lot to add another 30% to your profits.

If you're the marketing leader, you want to spend your time on high level strategy. Not on the daily implementation of lead-generating campaigns. And you don't want your Creators to feel like they're being micromanaged. **You don't want to <u>have</u> to micromanage them.**

Better results from your high level direction make a good case for your year end bonus.

Right now you might be doing precisely none of the things you read about in this book. And implementing two things you get from these pages can give that growth you need.

How much do you know about every role that falls under you?

Reading about sales, lead generation, positioning, and increasing your knowledge of how the roles beneath you work can also help you engage with that staff better and *drive them to improve their results.*

If you have a small sales team and it's been a long time since you actually got your hands dirty with sales yourself, what you read in this book helps realign you with the strategies they currently use. And should use. And helps you identify the gaps they have in their approach to sales for your business.

As a business owner, operator, or director of marketing people, this chapter holds benefits for your brain and your bank balance.

The financial benefits are obvious, yeah?

New sales leads = revenue growth.

But you probably overlook the benefits to your mental health. That comes from:

• Increased engagement of your workforce and lower staff turnover.

• Higher confidence in the effectiveness of your staff.

• Profits, pay increases.

When you understand - really understand - what your junior marketing manager contributes to lead generation or what your sales manager does to give their sales team more opportunities to work on, you can better oversee these job roles.

You have more reassurance you hired the right people to fill critical roles in the company.

You are also well equipped to audit their work, so you can push them to perform to the level you expect (if they aren't there now).

Get them a copy of this book and say "do this for the next 12 months."

And, of course, you're less stressed when your money is on the rise. So when you're flush, you handle those challenging moments at work gracefully.

Here's something else to think about.

B2B companies are starting to hire a new generation of marketing people. Digital natives. They know the tools. They read the blogs.

They don't have industry experience. And they might say they're excited to learn about the industry when you interview them for the job. But what they really want is a job that pays well.

You want them to care. Because caring leads to better insights into the industry, so they're better in their role, and of course they generate better results.

But they are usually just interested in getting by. Getting the paycheck.

With a few hours of reading, you have the tools to make them more industry savvy than they are (without them even really knowing it). They get more excited about the job because they're learning at a fast pace. And then they actually DO get excited about your industry. Without knowing it, they get aligned with your goals.

And we'll say it a million times - you will have the knowledge to evaluate their work and see their alignment with your goals crystalize.

The third C, Chris the Curator
For the sales or operations
manager

You're Chris the Curator

This book isn't just for your colleagues in marketing or the c-suite and ownership. It's for you too.

Want your sales team revitalized? Want them to be hunters instead of the passive order takers they might be turning into? This book shows your team the company is putting a genuine effort into getting them warm inbound leads.

Leads they can follow up with every day.

Some of you may have the resources to help you do this stuff. Graphic designers and writers, or a marketing intern, or a third party agency, that can create engaging and valuable assets based on the strategies and tactics detailed in these pages. With this book you'll learn *how to audit their work quickly, fairly, and confidently.*

But for those of you who don't, you can still have a huge impact on your inbound sales leads. Everything you need is here.

You can find a freelancer to get the bulk of the work done.

Then, we're going to show you how to use existing tools (AI and otherwise) right out of the box to do the things you aren't doing right now. Without taking on any more time consuming work. In fact, if you're looking for some good recommendations, you can see the tools we like right now at **www.jbbgi.com/tools.**

Don't let your business' internal limitations stop you from bringing your dream of plentiful inbound sales leads to life.

Remember - doing anything in this book, even if the design isn't as polished as the Forbes email that landed in your inbox this morning, will still generate exponentially more warm leads than you get today. Then more revenue. And that's what really matters.

You can read every page if you want. But you don't have to. Since this book is a choose your own adventure, all you have to do is <u>follow Chris the Curator's path</u>

- You'll get through the book in a couple sittings.

- You'll know what needs to get done.

- You'll know how to do it. Or who to pay to do it.

- And you'll know how to audit their work and give meaningful feedback with little effort.

The other thing is - by doing this well, you give yourself increased job security. Something you maybe never had before. You'll stop worrying about work when you're home with your family at the end of the day, because you know things are on the right trajectory.

Chapter 2

LEARN THE TRUTHS YOUR B2B COMPETITORS IGNORE.

So you know about the 3 C's. But there's something else you need to know before we get to the strategies. Know deep in your bones. Know and believe like you believe the most sacred truths in your life.

Your job is challenging. Because it's unique.

Whether you're Charles the Conductor, Claire the Creator, or Chris the Curator, your job is not the same as a B2C job. It's not the same as a B2B job in another industry.

You might be used to it by now. Like your body when you do the exact same thing at the gym every day.

But that sacred truth remains. Your job is challenging and unique.

Most people can't do what you do. Honestly, they can't. Give yourself a break and let that absorb.

But listen. The uniqueness of your job doesn't mean you have to reinvent sales lead generation from the ground up.

You can do the things we've done to help B2Bs capture a ton of leads. With a slight framework shift based on your industry, your expertise. Put your own lens on the things we talk about in this book.

In a way, your uniqueness doesn't matter. Because the challenge is just to capture sales leads so your business' revenue can grow. That's what it comes down to.

Why is B2B so challenging?

Because it's not B2C. We're not saying B2C is easy. But it's different. We're exposed to B2C marketing from the time we can look at a screen or understand the words on the radio.

And not in small quantities. It's our food, the places we get our food, the places beside the places we get our food. Our shoes, socks, pants. Our entertainment. Our schools. Most kids movies are just B2C marketing for toys.

Heck, George Lucas isn't a billionaire because Star Wars was a critical hit. He's a billionaire because he kept the rights to all Star Wars merchandising. And a lot of Star Wars swag has been sold to consumers since 1977.

But that's another story.

The point is, we're familiar with what B2C marketing looks like from a young age. We all speak that language. We can all tell good B2C marketing from bad.

Generating leads for B2B is different.

If you're a Creator (like a marketing manager) or Curator (a sales manager or operations manager) at a lab equipment manufacturer, for example, there's a good chance you never saw or heard of or even considered the possibility that a mercury analyzer was a real thing. Or that your life might one day revolve around increasing sales of rammers or surface sampling swabs.

And your prospects' pain points when they buy these things are totally foreign to you.

In B2C, it's easy to understand how sunglasses that float might help people who spend time on the water.

But in B2B, it's less intuitive to know that a spray dryer might reduce time wasted on sample prep so operators can spend more time on data analysis, which is actually what helps them move up in their careers.

Or a padfoot roller reduces costs associated with third party compaction testing on new road construction projects, so businesses can create more competitive quotes and win more contracts.

And how do you best communicate that knowledge once you possess it?

That's the challenge. And that's what this book teaches you to do.

And if you're a Conductor (the owner or operator of the business, the marketing director with staff working under you), you knew what you were getting into. You chose to be here rather than anywhere else. But that doesn't mean it's easy.

Most B2Bs don't have the luxury of a large specialized marketing team with brand marketers and performance marketers. But the truth is those silos aren't needed. They **are** a luxury. An expense of vanity.

What you need as a Conductor is your marketing team, or even your single marketing employee, or your 3rd party agency, doing the most valuable things properly. **And the knowledge to be sure they are.**

The challenges in the last few pages and the belief that you're totally unique is what fuels your imposter syndrome.

Your business might be unique. But your challenges are not. And we can band together to overcome all of this together.

You found your people here.

Why is this book timely?

We're at a tipping point. Maybe we always are.

But right now the B2B landscape is heaving, and it feels like something unique.

There's more competition than ever before. It's easier today than even 5 years ago to start and manage B2B businesses. From the digital tools to the digital communication methods we use with our customers and our supply chain, to third party fulfillment centers shipping our orders or drop shipping direct from the manufacturers.

This isn't because of the pandemic. This is not a post-pandemic business book. This is a 2020s to 2030s business book that teaches us how to adapt to the current environment. An environment that's been forming over the last two decades.

What are some of these new realities?

1. There are fewer and fewer in-house employees because they're turning side hustles into full time businesses. Or they're seeking greener pastures somewhere else.

It's increasingly hard to keep good staff. It's hard to find good staff when you have gaps in your current employee pool.

The ability for somewhat-experienced employees to start their own competing businesses is greater now than ever, and the willingness for employees to go off and start their own thing is equally great.

They're all fueled by the knowledge they absorbed working for you or your competitors. They have the tools to break into your prospect pool by capitalizing on that knowledge and using new digital tools.

If you had the choice early in your career in sales or marketing, would you have chosen to work at a consumer brand that you, your family, and your friends were all familiar with? Would you go back and make the same choice to work in a B2B business very few people have heard of before?

The allure to go sell expensive cupcakes or rock climbing shoes or kids' clothing is real, and **you're competing for the same workforce.**

So what does this mean? You just have to do more with less. The sooner we can accept the fact that the B2B industry cannot always hire whatever talent it needs on demand, at the same quality it used to get before, the sooner we can get on figuring out new ways to generate better results in-house with existing resources.

2. Your prospects today are more digital than they used to be and you need to capture your sales leads where they are.

Generation Z are more digital than Millennials and the next generation will be even more.

That doesn't mean building a VR showroom or setting up a tradeshow booth in the metaverse.

That means finding reliable ways to capture their attention and hold it long enough that they engage with your brand.

Actually, maybe that **does** mean building a VR showroom. If there's any tangible evidence it will achieve your goals

But we think **there are dozens of other ways to achieve your goals with a lower investment and higher return.** And we're going to show them to you.

3. Your prospects are less likely now to stay with the legacy suppliers their business has always worked with.

Your prospects want to have an impact on their own businesses.

That could come from something as simple as finding a new supplier. One that offers more value, better prices, better service. Whatever it might be. They want to bring a new idea to a stale environment and succeed with it.

That means two things for you.

First. **There are great opportunities to steal your competitors' customers.**

Second. **Your competitors have great opportunities to steal your customers.**

So you need to *simultaneously capture and retain better* than those competitors if you're going to increase profits.

These lead generation strategies will help you do that (of course it's up to you to communicate your value better than your competitors too).

4. Your prospects are less likely to turn to trade shows or flip through dead-tree trade publications.

Even with the excitement of returning to in-person events toward the end of 2022 and the first half of 2023, and attendance to trade shows staying stable (although diminished vs. attendance in 2018-2019), trade shows are not going to be what they were. Probably ever.

Because budgets have been reallocated to digital activities.

So they're doing more online. And you should be too.

Here's something everybody needs to think about

Supply chains aren't what they used to be and they will continue to fluctuate and shift and change as global events fluctuate and shift and change.

Your business needs to be as nimble as the supply chain allows.

That means **finding sales leads for what you actually have.**

What you *know* you can get.

What you *know* you can sell.

And uncovering the opportunities where your competitors fall short.

It might just be dumb luck that you happen to have supplies of products that are out of stock elsewhere. Or that your product replaces the usual product for scenario X or Y or Z.

Capture leads by identifying those scenarios and communicating through a permission asset and website merchandising (you'll learn exactly how to do this in the pages ahead).

And maybe you're reluctant to make these changes. Maybe all these reasons still don't make it feel worth the mental energy.

But what if you're thinking about the final phase of your business. Getting it ready to sell. **Maybe this is the last pivot you need to make to increase the valuation of your company and live the worry-free retirement you deserve.**

If you want to maximize the value of your exit from the business. This is how you do it this year.

If you want to move up in the company, this is how you show the top of the food chain you're ready for it.

If you want to get better at your job. If you want to be better than every B2B marketer out there, this is where you start.

If you want more sales leads and more revenue continue on with the next chapter to get started.

From this point on, there are only 6 steps you need to take to increase your sales leads for the rest of the year and beyond.

the
other guy

you

Chapter 3

STEP # 1. DEVELOP BETTER USPs THAN BRANDS 20X YOUR SIZE.

They help with the next 5 steps. And they're much easier than you think.

Spend time developing unique sales propositions (USPs). Some people call them unique selling propositions. That doesn't sound right to us. You feel the same way after reading them side-by-side, don't you?

Anyway.

What are they?

They're like elevator pitches for each solution you offer. A powerful message you can convey in just a few seconds. In words and visually. They have this magic that makes you the only viable option for your lead, prospect, customer.

Why do you need USPs?

Because most people make decisions in an instant. And you need a fast way to communicate the best value your product or service gives them. Those are your USPs.

Sculpting your USPs also helps you understand your own business better. Face realities and accept or work to change them.

Do you manufacture a line of hot plates because you saw other manufacturers were gouging customers and selling increasingly poor quality hot plates at increasingly high prices, and you found a way to use new materials to build a lower cost but better quality hot plate?

Or do you manufacture hot plates because there's a huge customer base and you wanted a piece of that action?

Either is fine. But the second one doesn't work as a USP. So you have to acknowledge it and move on to find something that works.

Oh. But **for the purpose of this book, here's the biggest reason you need USPs:**

You are going to generate leads with the help of a permission asset.

Good USPs help you make a <u>great</u> permission asset.

They help you give better instructions to the person making the permission asset (if you're Charles the Conductor or Chris the Curator).

They help you make merchandising assets easily (if you're Chris).

And they help you do everything more easily if you're Claire the Creator.

Without them, your permission asset will struggle to pick up steam.

What the heck is a permission asset? You'll get to that in about 7 pages. But first…

How many USPs do you need, and how many words should they be?

As many USPs as you can imagine!

If there are 12 ways you think your product differentiates itself from competing products, put those 12 USPs in neon lights.

The words should be short. Concise. Tight. And if you can say the same thing in 5 different ways, do it. Because different words appeal to different people. You want your prospects to see the words they relate to.

And they should lend themselves well to visual representation.

In most cases the USP is what you imagine sitting under a product image on your website. Attached to a small icon that stands out on your website or in your product brochure. Capturing that fleeting audience attention.

Often the goal of these USPs is to <u>allow you to produce a page with content that easily stands out to prospects and conveys your message at a glance</u>. To produce:

- A web page or email.

- A trifold brochure.

- Text on a trade show booth.

- Overlays on a video.

- Or, in our case, <u>a good permission asset</u>.

So how do you develop these USPs? What's the first step?

<u>Claire, Charles, and Chris all follow the same steps to make business-powering USPs.</u>

In fact, you've probably done this exercise already (maybe many times) in your business or in sales or marketing training. But you probably did it wrong. Well, not you. The person who walked you through it. So let's do it right today.

1.   Take out a sheet of paper. Old fashioned paper and pen stuff here.

2.   On the left hand side, record all your product's features. These are probably listed on the product detail pages on your website or the PDF you send to prospects. To most of your prospects these features mean almost nothing.

3.   On the right side of the paper, using your ink pot and quill, write down the benefit or benefits each feature gives your prospect. **The benefit is what matters to your customer.** The book you're reading right now <u>features</u> insights from B2B marketing experts. The <u>benefit</u> is that you get an easy roadmap to increased revenue and profits that you can implement today. Or, more boldly - *read this book and you'll make more money.*

Ok. Let's look at the most common example we see on most B2B websites.

"We offer fast delivery."

That's a feature. And in the world of Amazon, it's also expected. So it's weak.

We can whittle that down to a generic benefit - get delivery of the product tomorrow. But that's still weak.

Why is it **actually important to the customer?** What does that impact in their business?

• Maybe less instrument down time.
• Maybe less money wasted on overstocking.
• Maybe less space dedicated to hazardous material storage.
• Maybe they can place smaller orders more often because that's important for cash flow in the business.

As a business statement, it could be something like: *Right size your facility.*
Don't waste budget on excess inventory and the space to hold it. We keep it for you.

Or: *Don't order parts until your customer signs the contract. You can still start*
production tomorrow thanks to our fast local logistics.

But is the "why" the same for everyone in your target audience or is it
different based on the type of industry they're in or the job role you're
speaking to?

Many B2B companies have a basic breakdown of customers, industry, or
company type (public, private, EDU, government, local, international,
whatever). Because you (or the person in your role before you) followed email
marketing best practices for the past 20 years, your list is segmented in such a
way. And you can use this segmentation to your advantage.

If you don't have access to this kind of segmentation, you could look at
websites or LinkedIn profiles related to the last 50 sales the business has made.

It's valuable to know about the audience because the "why" and even the
benefits of the features from your equipment differ based on the type of
industry your customer is in.

And you can even go further. The individual human engaging with your
business sees different benefits depending on their job role.

So, do we write one USP in an attempt to appease all industries and job roles?
You're 6,199 words into this book right now, so you can probably guess the
answer is a very loud **no.**

Now we (and by we, we mean you) want to do some mapping.

Here's exactly how:

Record the various industries and the job titles in your contact database on another piece of paper. If you don't have that information, guess. Spot check your customers' websites (like we mentioned above, based on your last 50 sales). Do the same to Linkedin accounts.

You're going to map the USP statements to each industry and job role, and customize a specific phrasing of the benefit for that role. Then add a new column to explain why that benefit matters to that role.

It'll look something like this in the end:

Feature	Benefit	Industry	Job	Specific Benefit	Why?
K-Thermocouple	Best Available temp control	Pharma	Lab Manager	Lose less sample and save R&D budget to make balancing your costs easier	Because budget management sucks
K-Thermocouple	Best Available temp control	Pharma	Lab Tech	Save more sample so you can collect more data per spray run	Because the data is what their job is about

Do this and your business positioning, product positioning, or service positioning will be better than almost every business in your B2B niche.

"But there are huge brands in my niche and they have all the money and resources to do this better than me."

Wrong, friend. Wrong!

Here's how Bombardier, with vast creative resources, positions its Challenger 350 Business Jet.

- **Smooth ride.** An optimally balanced aircraft design provides you with an exceptionally smooth ride from takeoff to touchdown.

- **Largest cabin.** Sit back and relax in the largest cabin in its class. Featuring exquisite finishes and sleek styling, a flat floor design and safe access to baggage at all times, it delivers high style and comfort without compromise.

- **Quietest cabin.** Minimize noise to maximize comfort in the quietest cabin in its class. Equipped with a standard entry door acoustic curtain and galley pocket door, the aircraft's sound suppressing design ensures optimal productivity and relaxation in flight.

- **Lowest direct operating costs.** Through longer maintenance intervals, low parts cost and increased efficiency, operators benefit from the lowest in-class operating costs making the Challenger 350 aircraft a wise decision

- **Highest reliability.** With its outstanding dispatch reliability, the Challenger 350 aircraft was designed to deliver peace of mind.

We know the audience is corporate flight departments and charter operations. Bombardier stopped at the features and never got to the actual benefits. If you were Bombardier, you might say this to charter operations:

- **Coax nervous flyers from your competitors.** The unique balancing of this aircraft gives nervous flyers a smoother ride. So they choose you over competitors.

- **Book higher-value clients who work on the go.** A larger cabin than comparable aircrafts gives high-value clients more space to work and unwind on the move. Something your competitors can't offer.

- **Capture more frequent business travelers.** The relentless hum of most aircraft gets in the way of business calls and deep work. Frequent business travelers prefer quiet spaces where they control their surroundings. With the Challenger 350, it's your advantage.

- **Earn more profit with each flight.** With longer maintenance intervals, low parts cost and increased efficiency, you can increase your profits without raising your prices.

- **Win more business through your reputation.** Outstanding dispatch reliability means your clients miss fewer arrivals. Maybe they never miss an arrival time again!

When you have a collection of USPs that make you want to buy from your business, you're ready to rock and roll with your primary sales lead generating asset. Something we call a permission asset.

Your USPs will help guide your decision making over the next 50+ pages.

If you're a Creator, you have the most foundational, raw value your customers care about at your fingertips. You will use this extensively when creating your permission asset (that's what comes next). And we will show you the exact steps to follow as you do it.

If you're a Curator or Conductor, the person you put in charge of creating your permission asset content has clear direction on the value they need to convey in the content they create. We'll show you precisely how to prepare them, direct them, and audit their output with minimal effort.

Indeed this is where your paths diverge based on your position in the business. Of course you are free to read every word that covers the rest of this book. But you can also stick to your path - Creators, Curators, Conductors. And you'll be generating sales leads like Steven King generates nightmares.

Chapter 4

STEP # 2. CREATE SOMETHING YOUR PROSPECTS CAN'T LIVE WITHOUT.

You're going to create, or direct the creation, of a lead magnet (we call it a permission asset). It will drive your increase in sales leads this year.

Now we're going to walk you through a straightforward workflow to create the thing at the heart of your lead generating efforts. It's called a permission asset. And if anybody outside your business wants it (and you bet your favorite bottle of tequila they will), they're going to have to give a little something for it.

What is a permission asset (PA) & how does it generate leads?

Most visitors to your website never wave to say hello. They don't strike up a conversation just to chat. They don't share their contact information with you.

Only about 2.25% of the website traffic B2B equipment manufacturers or suppliers generate will convert into a lead by:

- Completing a form on your website (1.1%).

- Emailing the info@ address from your footer (0.15%)

- Calling the phone number from the header or contact page of your website (1%).

How do you compare?
Here's the quickest way to find out.

1. Open your Google Analytics dashboard.

2. Look at your total number of website visitors over a defined time period (in the image below, we picked 90 days because it's a simple preset in the Google Analytics dropdown menu).

3. Then open up your CRM and find the number of sales leads over the same defined time period.

4. Divide the # of sales leads by the # of website visitors. Maybe you get a number like 0.0125.

5. Multiply by 100 and that's the percentage of your website visitors converting to leads.

That's your number.

So how can you increase it? How can you possibly follow up with them if they don't inquire about something today? How can you make sure they didn't overlook important info that would help them convert to sales? How can you give them value and improve your relationship to the point where they trust you?

This is where we talk about the permission asset.

The goal of a permission asset is to increase the percentage of visitors saying hello and sharing their contact information. It's an easy way to get way more sales leads than you get today.

At a very high level, a permission asset is something the visitors to your website are willing to exchange their contact information to get. They complete a form, they get the handy guide to cleanroom particle counters, or rotary evaporators, or slump test equipment, or whatever you manufacture or distribute.

This permission asset builds the foundation for all future marketing efforts to that prospect (and others like them).

And you want that permission asset to offer knowledge targeted toward someone at the top of a sales funnel.

What sort of questions or concerns does a prospective customer have when they begin their journey toward purchasing the equipment or services you provide?

These are the perfect questions to answer in your permission asset. This way you know you will attract targeted and qualified prospects. Your content is only helpful to people with an intent to purchase and these are the people to focus your energy on.

But why do you need ANOTHER step in the sales process?

<u>Because</u> prospects are visiting your website right now and you don't know who more than 97% of them are. That means the business you own or work in is currently surviving on less than 3% of the sales it *could*, in theory, make. Imagine capturing another full %. Or two.

This is another way to get prospects to reveal themselves to you. It's always better to give them more opportunities to identify themselves, and in the process you can get them excited about what you do for them.

And you get to control the narrative with those prospects. You get to influence the specs that go into an RFQ. You don't lose your audience to BS from another manufacturer or supplier.

If you work in an industry where there is a lot of knowledge to be shared, why not get something in exchange for the knowledge you already have?

It's a very small commitment for any prospect visiting your website to enter their email address in exchange for something that can:

- help them save money

- or make a better purchase

- or look better to their boss

- or make their staff happier and more likely to stay with the business

- Or helps them compress time

This is the ideal strategy for *challenger brands*. You're not the industry leader in your product segment <u>right now</u>. If you were, you probably wouldn't be reading this. Because this is one of the strategies that puts you in that leadership position.

Aside from getting prospects to share their information, think about it what it does to the positioning of the next person they come in contact with at your company.

When you go to the doctor they don't try to sell you a prescription. You go to them because they are the expert in this space and you seek their experience and expertise to figure out what you need.

The permission asset positions your staff as the doctors with the expertise to make educated, valuable recommendations. Maybe life-changing (at least work-life-changing) recommendations.

What type of content can be used as a PA?

Here's the main thing you need to be able to say about your permission asset once it's written and designed.

This is helpful to my prospective customers.

Fill it with knowledge you find yourself sharing on sales calls. Knowledge you wish you had earlier in your career. Knowledge that's not common.

And knowledge that is. If you're Chris the Curator for example, you don't need to have unique knowledge. You just need to have smart positioning (and you already worked on that when you developed your USPs in this book's first activity). That smart positioning is your unique angle. And your unique angle is the best way to engage with end users.

Make it comprehensive, so you can confidently and persuasively use it to influence a prospective customer to exchange contact info for it.

Want more about the type of content you can pour into this? Flip ahead to page 32.

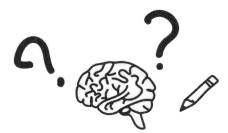

How do you write a permission asset?

First choose what type of content you will write or have written for you: This could be in the form of:

1. **A thought leadership article (want some specifics about this? Flip to page 40).**
2. **A case study (you might not have done interviews before. That's alright, get some tips for yourself or your Creator on page 63).**
3. **A buyer's guide (but not just any buyer's guide - more about this on page 70).**

We recommend these three most often.

There are others, like whitepapers and application notes and eBooks. But in a way, those are all sort of stale takes on the three options we recommend above (thought leadership, case study, buyer's guide).

Why don't we think a buyer's guide is as stale as a whitepaper? You'll see below

From here, you can do two things.

- Look for ideas first
- Or choose the permission asset type first, and jump to that section below.

First, we'll show you where to find ideas.

Then, we'll explain what each type of permission asset is, and show you how exactly to write/create/direct the creation of it.

Having a hard time thinking of what your first permission asset will talk about? Want to know where you can look for ideas?

Here's a high level look at 13 places you can find easy subjects to write about.

1. Google autocompletion in the top search bar of your web browser (just start typing about your product or industry and see what Google recommends).

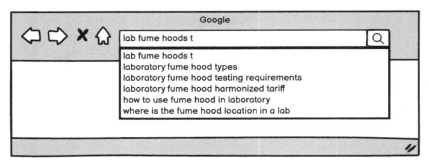

2. Google search results suggestions (all the way at the bottom of the page when you type a search)

Related searches :

Q benchtop fume hood

Q labconco fume hood

Q fume hood uses in laboratory

Q chemical fume hood

Q fume hood manufacturers

Q laboratory fume hood price

Q ductless fume hood

Q fume hood canada

3.   Ahrefs.

   a.   We use Ahrefs for lots of reasons. One of these reasons is *finding questions related to B2Bs we work with.*

   b.   After you sign up, you can find questions related to your query thusly:

       i.   Click on Keywords Explorer.

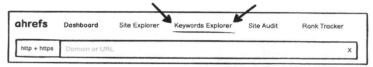

      ii.   Type in your words and hit enter.

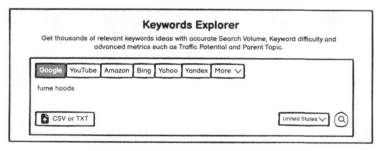

     iii.   The results page includes questions people search for related to the words you typed in the previous step.

Keywords ideas

Test match		Questions	
fume hoods	900	how do fume hoods work	90
fume hoods are used to	150	what are fume hoods are used for	80
lab fume hoods	100	what do fume hoods protect you from	30
used fume hoods	100	what do fume hoods do	20
how do fume hoods work	90	what is the osha regulatory statement concerning "face velocity" of air flow for safety fume hoods?	20
View all 855 >		View all 113 >	

c.   And now you have ideas to pay your Creator to write about.

4.   Search on YouTube

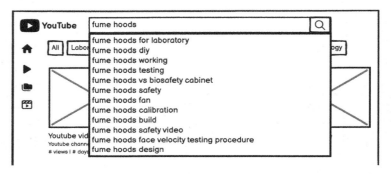

5.   Search on Reddit. Even if you've never used the website before, just throw your keyword into the search and browse thousands of conversations where people have mentioned it. There's a more detailed rundown of how to use Reddit efficiently on page 52.

a.   Here you'll get unfiltered discussions about the subject. It's as close as you can get to listening in to your customers with top secret but totally legal spy gear.

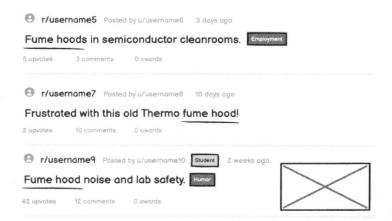

6. Join LinkedIn and Facebook groups relevant to the industry you sell into.

    a. Just type a keyword or series of keywords into the search bar.
    b. Click on the groups button that appears in the search results.
    c. Join the group.
    d. Scroll through the post history and see what folks are thinkin'.

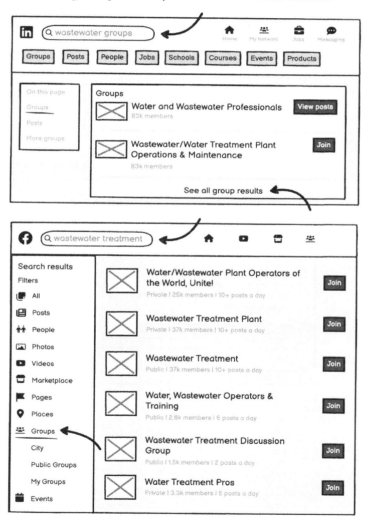

7. Search on Google for product reviews. For your own products, for competitors' products, and for the products your customers sell to their own customers. In the reviews, you can often find insights into challenges those audiences face.

8. Look for questions people are asking in industry-specific forums your target audience would belong to.

   a. Like ResearchGate.net for scientists

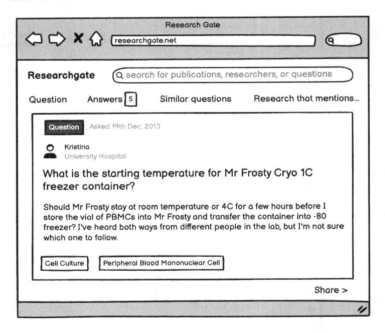

9. Look on general forums like Medium.com and Stackexchange.com where people are asking questions about technology in your industry.

10. Search your product category on Kickstarter.com and see what innovations (or pipedreams) people are working on in your area.

11. Look at what your competitors say on their websites and in their own permission assets.

    a.   Maybe you can correct them.

    b.   Maybe you can go further than them.

    c.   Maybe you can aggressively contradict them.

12. Find the **secret insights** in Google Shopping.

    a.   Search for your product category on Google.

    b.   In the search results page, click Shopping.

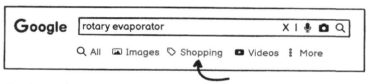

    c.   Sort by product rating.

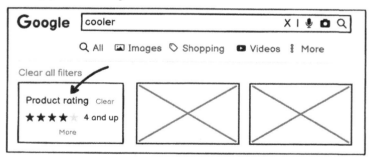

    d.   Then you can click on the product reviews to see what people are saying.

    e.   Even if the content you want to create isn't centered around a product, by searching products from your subject area you uncover reviews that give insights into problems you can solve in your permission asset.

You might already have things to repurpose into a valuable permission asset

Most B2Bs have plenty of existing material to turn into a permission asset, that prospects will want to read. And there are different sources depending on whether you're a manufacturer or distributor.

Manufacturers look for:

· A talk someone from the business did at a conference - notes, recording, powerpoint. Whatever!

· An article the business wrote for a 3rd party.

· A webinar from two years ago that's gathering dust.

· Internal product planning documents that can spin into a compelling story.

· Conversations that happened via email through the sales process with a client.

· Meeting notes or other internal notes from the time your company switched filter providers, or rubber providers, or thermocouple providers, etc...

· An old YouTube or Vimeo video.

Distributors look for:

· Everything your manufacturer counterparts look for, plus...

· Product literature provided by the manufacturer.

· Downloadable content that already exists on the manufacturer website.

· Videos the manufacturer uploaded to YouTube.

Or it might be something else.

Open up your Google docs or search Office365 for keywords.

In the spring of 2024 we searched for "testimonial" in our Google docs. It turned up a document with short testimonials we'd forgotten about from several years ago. We reached out to the businesses named in those stale testimonials and half of them agreed to a chat, leading to several unexpected and valuable case study permission assets!

Or maybe it's not an existing document or creative asset of some sort. Maybe it's a person.

Who do you have that you could leverage to create content from?

Your orbit is full of people with unique insights that could help you create valuable content - whether it's thought leadership, a case study, or a buying guide.

So who are these resource-rich bodies floating around you?

1. A sales person in your business who is passionate about a specific market segment.

2. A customer you have encountered repeatedly who uses your products to solve a key challenge

3. An engineer who designs products you sell.

4. A marketing manager who spends lots of time evaluating the competition.

So those are all the places you can look for ideas.

And now, the types of permission assets and how to bring them to life.

Chapter 5

ESTABLISH YOURSELF AS AN INDUSTRY VISIONARY.

Permission asset type #1. **Thought leadership.**

These can be written by anyone who has passion for the solution. The challenges your products or services solve for your customers.

They don't require deeply technical knowledge - unless you want to choose a deeply technical subject for your business or your figurehead to be a thought leader on.

Why is a thought leadership article good?

- You don't need the same level of detail or hands-on product experience as you would to write an application note or white paper.

- You don't need permission from any customers to write this like you would with a case study.

- You don't need to collaborate with anyone, really. Just write or assign a writer to build with what you know.

So what is a thought leadership article?

Your opinion. The edgier the headline/subject, the better! You can always soften your radical opinion by giving the popular opinion a fair shake in the permission asset.

You or your colleagues talk to customers all the time. You hear about their challenges and how people overcome them. **And you have an opinion about which one you think is best.**

If everyone else has the same opinion, it wouldn't be worth writing about (although there's an argument to be made about the power of the echo chamber). But we're talking about leadership, so we want to find a stance on a topic that is slightly off the beaten path and maybe the less popular opinion.

But wait a second. That sounds like clickbait.

Well yeah, it sort of is.

Get rid of that negative connotation though. Call it click enticement. Click magnetism. Clexcellence.

You *really* need people to stop scrolling, whether your content shows up in their inbox or social media feeds or through your web page.

They need that topic, that headline, that subject line, that image on social media to gain their interest.

How can you do this?

A.   You have to look deeply at the benefits your product or solution gives your customer. Why is it important to them. Why is it important **right now? What is going on in your industry that makes them care about this? What is going on with the supply chain? With materials and designs? With staffing?** Why should they solve their problems this way?

Your thought leadership is not just relevant, but it's timely.

B.   Your thought leadership content <u>might not be focused on the primary business challenge your company solves</u> for your customers. Maybe it's a tertiary challenge people just aren't talking about enough.

Here's an example from our business.

Oh boy, we're going to talk about laboratory freezers!

You're a lab freezer manufacturer.

At the start of the pandemic, as new vaccines were developed and distributed across the world, the public started learning about the cold chain. The network of cold spaces and cold transportation that moves temperature-sensitive medicines (and more) from manufacturing facilities to grocery stores and clinics and retirement homes and so on.

The primary benefit of any freezer used for science is that it keeps samples of science stuff at the consistent, low temperature needed so scientists can do more science stuff later. Or so the science stuff that's already done doesn't spoil.

So there are some easy benefits to identify. Your work doesn't spoil. Your business doesn't lose money. You don't have to recall product. You don't lose your job when a large batch of product spoils. All from making sure your lab workers have sufficient, quality freezer space.

And there are more things too.

Maybe yours has some technology like compressors that are insulated better than your competitors. And that technology creates a benefit to the customer - lower energy consumption or less heat dumping or something. This is a unique sales proposition as well. It just needs a little massaging (you can learn more about this in the chapter on USPs that starts back on page 18).

But is it enough to create a whole thought leadership stance around? That depends on how creative you can get. But our answer is yes. Yes!

Once you start peeling back the onion, you can explore all the other alternative solutions to reducing the customer's labs energy consumption and decreasing risk. You could form the opinion that no lab should buy any equipment that doesn't achieve this level of energy efficiency because anything less eats too far into profits. Or that no lab should have fewer than 2 backup freezers to avoid sudden sample loss due to freezer failure.

And you can highlight pain points for other stakeholders in the laboratory.

- If your lab uses an old or budget-priced wall of freezers, you're contributing more to climate change than other labs. That doesn't line up with your corporate goals.
- The looming energy crisis means the cost of energy will skyrocket, and you'll be paying far more in the long run if you opt for a budget-priced set of freezers now. So your operating budget can't handle the long term implications of a less efficient freezer.
- You are employed because you are the steward of expensive samples. Your job is to protect those samples. Those samples feed your family. Protect those samples!

Combine that with a title like Pick the Wrong Lab Freezer and Penguins Will Suffer and BAM!, you have something that will stop people in their scroll and get them to engage with your brand. You have their attention to tell your story. It's timely and it's relevant to the industry.

And of course your story positions your product above all your competitors.

Can we get to the *how do you write it* part already?!

Alright, fine.

Claire, Chris, and Charles - you all start by drafting an outline. And the start of the start is a mind map (although Charles has a different approach to this, which you can learn about on page 57).

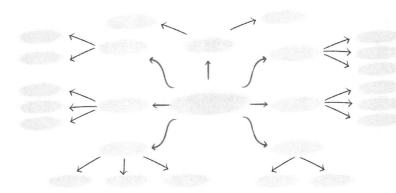

So here's how you do it.

1. Put the problem you're trying to solve or the opinion you want to argue in the middle of the page. Draw your best grade school circle around it.

2. Write 4-5 possible solutions or supporting facts around your central circle. Circle them up too.

3. Repeat the process again with your new circles. Write down other supporting facts, other problems, other solutions.

    a. Don't be afraid to write bad ones. They help you iron out the form your final piece of content will take. You can even use the bad ones comically in your thought leadership permission asset. Your audience is human. We like jokes.

4. Decide when you're done. A full page makes it easier for you to write. So when your page is full, you can move on.

A mind map is also a neat collaborative tool.

If there are people around you in the business who are invested in the success of this permission asset, get them to contribute to the mind map.

They might have ideas you don't. Their ideas may lead to more of your own ideas. Your ideas might give them more ideas.

And all of this makes it easier for you to complete your task.

Claire the Creator - here's what you do next

Take your mind map and transform it into a written draft. Call it a manuscript or a blog even. Which might sound intimidating. But all you have to do is open a Google doc or Word doc and start writing. There's nothing fancy about it.

Make it orderly and logical.

Oh wait, you already made it orderly and logical. So this actually takes no time at all.

The title of your document = **the central bubble in your mind map.**

The section headings (use H1 tags to automatically give yourself an index on the left side of your Google doc) = **the first level of bubbles around the middle.**

The subheadings within each section (use H2 tags) = **the other bubbles with the wider orbits.**

Just like that you have all your sections organized in a Google doc. You have a table of contents that's dynamically generated. You have all the answers to the questions readers will ask. All the points of interest.

You have bones! Strong, healthy bones.

But you need more than bones.

Hot tip for Creators who want to flesh out ideas more easily

With somewhere around 1,000 permission assets under our belts, we find some sections of content are easier to talk about than write about.

Generally, for us (it might be different for you, but there's no reason you shouldn't try new things) talking about content that's more qualitative in nature is easier than writing about it.

Ideas can flow more naturally. Conversationally. They have a higher likelihood of landing on the paper (or the screen that's still formatted as a white square of paper) like you hear them in your head.

So what's the easiest way to <u>dictate</u> thoughts into a piece of written content?

1. Load up a Google doc from your phone.
2. Move your eyes slightly to the bottom right of the screen where you'll notice a tiny microphone icon.
3. Tap it.
4. Blab away!

This stuff you're reading right now? Dictated. We tested the process with a Google Pixel and were so impressed with the accuracy and voice controls that we both ditched our iPhones and joined team Google.

So if you were sitting with us at the time of writing, you'd see a Google document open on the laptop screen, connected to a projector so we can both dictate comfortably while eating fiery samosas in the office lounge. You'd see the same Google doc open on a phone resting on a side table between us. And you'd see these words appearing in real time with a high degree of accuracy.

Yeah, it's not groundbreaking stuff. Dragon NaturallySpeaking was released in 1997. At the time it was a great way to get essays done at the last possible minute, after 2 months of procrastinating in high school.

But those essays were full of grammatical errors and straight up incorrect words.

Today, it's so much better.

Quantitative stuff - data, surveys, improvements in budget use, process efficiency upgrades - doesn't work the same for us. It might for you. But if you're struggling with it, try this:

- Create bullet points, 2-3 sentences long.

- Then figure out a way to connect your bullet points with interesting observations or supporting information later.

- Don't let the quantitative stuff slow down your flow with the qualitative stuff.

Let's talk about the flow

Not the literal flow of what you're writing. The flow state. The zone. The place where you do amazing things.

You've seen or read interviews with athletes who talk about the world dropping away when they perform at their peak. You can find interviews online with athletes who perform extraordinary feats. Michael Jordan and Kobe Bryant. Floyd Mayweather. Chris Sharma. Miguel Cabrera. Michael Schumacher. Messi. Ronaldo. The Great One. Peyton Manning.

All they are in that moment is the moment.

Here's a 139 word story about that.

In the 1992 NBA finals, Michael Jordan drained six 3-pointers in the first quarter against the Portland Trail Blazers. But he wasn't known as a great outside shooter. That season, he only made about one in every four attempts.

So he's just taking these shots. Crushing the Trail Blazers. And he hits the 6th. He turns and catches Magic Johnson's eye (who was working as a commentator at the time). And shrugs. Not just any shrug. The Shrug. Proper noun.

Why shrug?

Here's what he said after.

"I was in the groove. I was in the rhythm. It's something I can't really explain. The rim seemed like a big old huge bucket, and I can't miss it. I looked at Marvin and Magic and those guys and what can I say? It's not me, it's just the moment."

It's dramatic and super cool. It seems unique and special because it was on such a grand stage.

But the truth is we're all capable of it. And we use it repeatedly every day. It's just that most of us don't make a big fuss about it. And sometimes (read: always) it's in a more mundane scenario than His Airness.

When the ideas are coming smooth and fast, you want to keep it going. You're in your own flow state.

Thinking too hard about the perfect way to position your data in your writing at this point will stop your momentum and make everything else you're writing more challenging.

It's why MJ shrugged. He didn't know what he was doing. He was just doing it. His knowledge and experience and skills were working together in harmony. He wasn't stopping to think about his 27% 3-point-shooting average on the season.

(And since you're reading this book, you're getting the knowledge and taking a short cut straight to the skills).

So make bullet points about the quantitative stuff. And keep flowing with the rest.

When you've completed the content under all the layers of subheadings, and your word count is between 1,500 and 3,800, you're done the writing.

Now you're on to the design.

You're going to use Canva to design your permission asset.

You'll build these quickly on an A4-sized document and save the completed file as a standard PDF.

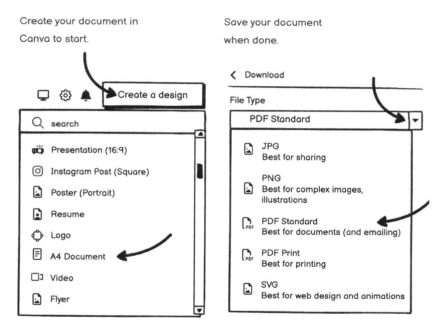

A lot of personal choice goes into the design of a permission asset of any type. The pictures you use. The font. The colors.

But you CAN follow some general design guidelines to make this process fast and easy, whether you make a thought leadership piece (like we've been talking about here so far), a buying guide, or a case study.

When you get to the buying guide section or the case study section of this book in the next few pages, we'll send you right back here to follow the same design guide for those permission assets.

Here's a quick checklist for everything your permission asset design needs:

1. A cover page.
2. An index page.
3. A footer with your logo, website, and the current page number.
4. Images throughout.
5. All the words from the Google doc.

When you boil it down, it's not all that much. And when you have simple wireframe templates to follow, it's very easy to get your work done quickly.

So here are your wireframes.

The cover of your permission asset

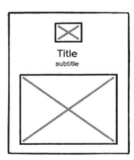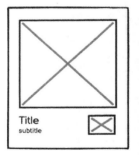

The index or table of contents

Table of contents

page title 1

page title 2

    sub page title 3

page title 4

page title 5

    sub page title 6

The body pages

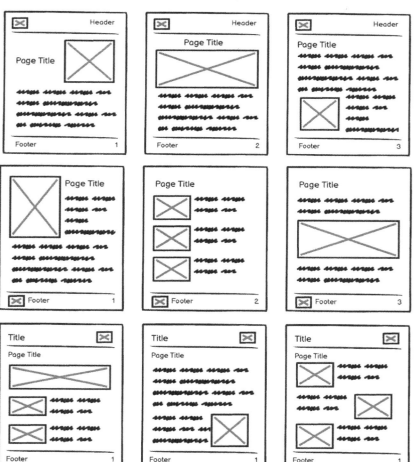

This gives your readers plenty of variety to keep them engaged as they read your content. And Canva's drag-and-drop design makes your job fast - and it's almost impossible to make errors (so you don't have much to worry about).

Once your design is done, you're happy with the way it all looks, you can skip down to page 88 for your next steps.

Chris the Curator - here's how you can create your thought leadership permission asset

You make a mind map, just like Claire the Creator. Scroll back to page 44 for quick instructions about how to do this.

You can't get around doing this, even if it feels like a timesink. Because it will *drastically improve the efficiency of the rest of your thought leadership creation.*

When your mind map is complete, you use content available online to populate each section (remember - each of the bubbles in your mind map can be the heading in a section of your permission asset).

Remember - every word you wrote surrounding your central problem or opinion in the mind map can form a subsection of the thought leadership permission asset.

But you don't have to shred your brain and write every subsection yourself.

You can look for the content you're going to use, which you will paraphrase or rewrite with ChatGPT, in four familiar places. There are other places (we gave you a high level look at these on page 32), but these four are low-energy and high-return, even for niche subjects.

1. On Reddit. There's a Reddit community for everything.

    a. Go to the Reddit home page and click in the search bar.

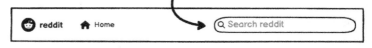

    b. Type your 1st subheading into the search bar.

c. **Don't look for your answers in these results. Just look for groups (subreddits) where discussions related to your search are happening. Join those subreddits.**

d. After you join a subreddit, it appears in your subreddits menu. You can also do searches in that specific group, so you filter out all the chaff that appears in site-wide searches. You know your search results in these groups will turn up relevant results.

Results for "freezer" in a site-wide search include:

r/username1 Posted by u/username2 2 months ago

Who leaves the ice cream box uncovered in the freezer?

16.4k upvotes   3.1k comments   0 awards

r/username3 Posted by u/username4 7 days ago

I think we should change 'Could he beat Goku?' for 'Could he beat Black Freezer?' Discussion

1.0k upvotes   181 comments   0 awards

r/username5 Posted by u/username6 22 days ago

Family of Arby's manager found dead in freezer sues fast food giant

dailymail.co.uk/news

2.6k upvotes   260 comments   0 awards

Results for "freezer" in a subreddit dedicated to medical lab professionals:

r/username7 Posted by u/username8 2 days ago

Which laboratory fridges and freezers are good? (And which to avoid?)

4 upvotes   4 comments   0 awards

r/username9 Posted by u/username10 5 days ago

Lab vs Retail - 20C Freezer

1 upvote   5 comments   0 awards

r/username11 Posted by u/username12 8 days ago

DMSO question...

3 upvotes   6 comments   0 awards

r/username13 Posted by u/username14 9 days ago

Can I repurpose expired urine sample containers? Jobs/Work

1 upvote   5 comments   0 awards

r/username15 Posted by u/username16 10 days ago

Anyone storing vaccine in the lab deep freezer

8 upvotes   8 comments   0 awards

e.   The relevant results are often lost in a sea of irrelevant results, so joining and searching in relevant subreddits helps you find the good stuff.

f.   Now that you can search relevant subreddits quickly, you can search for keywords and phrases related to your permission asset subsections.

g.   You can copy and paste the content from threads on Reddit into your permission asset. You can reword and add your own thoughts. You can paste it into ChatGPT and ask the AI to rewrite it with more insights, or shorten it, or turn it into a poem, or generate opposing viewpoints.

2.   On YouTube. The content is there and you, Curator, can curate it.

a.   Search for combinations of the phrase, question, problem you're creating words for.

b.   Use an AI tool like Otter.AI to capture the words in videos that serve your needs.

c.   Paste the text captured by Otter.AI or your preferred transcription tool into your Google doc.

d.   You should give credit to the source video if you keep the content as it is. If you just use it as inspiration and change it enough, say half, there might not be a need to link back.

e.   Hot tip: don't forget to look at the comments of the videos you use to help create your permission asset. There can be insightful additions from the niche community the video was made for, and you can use those to make your content more complete.

3. On LinkedIn. Your customers are talking about everything you care about.

    a. Similar to Reddit, you're going to find groups where the subjects you care about in your permission asset might be talked about.

    b. Start with high level industry groups, like:

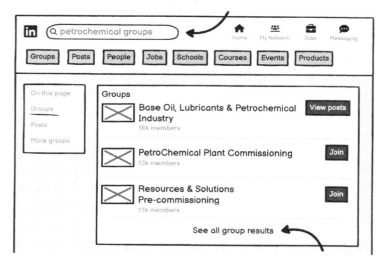

    c. Then niche down and see if any groups exist for specific applications related to your permission asset, like:

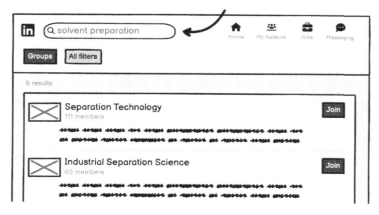

d. Once you're accepted to a group, you can search for posts containing keywords in the group. Just go to the group and use the search bar at the top left of the page.

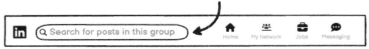

e. You can take the words from a relevant post and ask ChatGPT to rewrite it for you. Expand on it. Add context of your own.

4. On Google. Obviously.

a. There is already an impossible volume of content available online.
b. Put your questions to Google and see what comes up.
c. Phrase it several different ways to see the different results you get.
d. If you borrow any content from a blog or a report, it's good to link back to it from your permission asset, giving credit to the original published work.

You already did the tough work of getting your positioning right (and if you didn't, you can go back to page 18 and make some magic). These four sources can give you all the formed ideas and content you need to create the text of a valuable permission asset without spending long hours writing.

Then you need to design it.

And don't worry if you don't have any design background.

There's a walkthrough in this book you can use to quickly lay out your permission asset using Canva (an incredibly easy online graphic design tool) and simple wireframes we've provided.

It'll take you less than 2 hours from start to finish.

And after that, you'll have your first ever thought leadership permission asset. Your next steps resume on page 88.

Charles the Conductor - this part is for you

You're the boss.

You probably don't have the time or desire to build a mind map. But you need it done. So…

There are two ways to get this done while leveraging knowledge and experience from inside your business.

#1 Make the mind map the first deliverable you ask for from someone else. Your sales manager. Your best sales person. Your director of business development. A long-term applications engineer. But not someone in your marketing department.

Go to **www.jbbgi.com/mindmap** for a quick mind map template you can download.

#2 Get ChatGPT to interview you and output the mind map based on your answers.

Sounds daunting? Not if you can copy and paste the prompts we would use for this.

You can copy and paste the prompts from **www.jbbgi.com/aiprompts**

Once you have your mind map, you can offload the bulk of the work to a Creator.

If you don't have a marketing team or person available, or your favorite B2B marketing agency on retainer, you can find a freelancer for hire on **www.upwork.com**, **www.fiverr.com**, or **www.guru.com**.

If you do, you're a step ahead.

You don't have to write any complicated instructions to your Creator. You can just take the section of this book dedicated to Claire the Creator and copy+paste it to them verbatim.

You can find those words on our website here
- **www.jbbgi.com/templates**

The only thing you <u>do</u> need to put time into is giving your Creator all the contextual information you think they need to get your positioning right.

About positioning

When you're paying someone to write a thought leadership piece, it's almost guaranteed they don't have the same experience as you. And they won't write from the same perspective as you would, even if your mind map is super detailed.

But you want the content to reflect your values, not theirs. So you have to hammer home the position you want to come from.

For example, let's say you're a manufacturer and the ultimate goal of your content is to sell more fume hoods. You've chosen to commission a thought leadership piece. But it's **not about why your fume hoods are better**. Because that's not thought leadership.

Rather, your thought leadership piece is about why HEPA filter replacements are overpriced industry-wide. Or how a certain type of motor should be the industry standard for X, Y and Z reasons. Or how B2Bs in your industry can increase profits with these supplier relationship guidelines in place.

Your position needs to be baked into center bubble of the mind map.

If you want a **buying guide** from your Creator (more about buying guides on page 73), don't ask them to write about your fume hoods. Don't ask them to write about why your fume hoods are better. Write simply about features and benefits of fume hoods - features yours happen to have. And box out your competitors by making elements of your fume hoods the most important elements of any fume hood.

Don't let Claire the Creator say "our fume hoods have XYZ filters which are the best filters available." They should say, "reliable air filtration keeps your operators safe and significantly reduces sample waste or testing anomalies due to cross contamination. Fume hoods using XYZ filters are best in these scenarios." Yours happen to have that filter, but you're not saying BUY FROM US (which puts customers off). You're saying what's important and easing them into your sales proposition.

If you want a **case study** made (more on case studies on page 63), don't position it as *"Here's how WE helped this other business solve a problem."* Explicitly tell Claire to position it as *"This other business had this problem. And here's how this other business solved it with our help."*

Give your Creator a week to turn around the text for the first permission asset they're working on. Make it 4 days next time.

How to review your Creator's work.

When Claire the Creator submits their work for your review, you can easily compare their submission to the mind map you provided. That's the first thing you should do.

Then, as you read through the submitted content, keep these things in mind:

1. Are there any blocks of text that seem too long and daunting to me? (because they'll definitely feel daunting to your prospects).

2. Are there any blocks of text that could be reformatted as bullet points?*

3. Are there any blocks of text that could be pulled out into a graphic?*

4. **Does this respect the context and positioning you identified when you asked the Creator to do this work?**

Your Creator should already have these built into their submission. But if they haven't, it's an easy opportunity for you to show them you're paying attention, you know what you're doing, and you want more from them.

If the work is acceptable, the next step is getting it designed into a downloadable PDF.

If you have a designer on your marketing team, nice!

If you don't, you can go back to your favorite B2B marketing agency, or freelancers on Upwork of Fiverr or Guru and find one.

You can also get any millennial or post-millenial to give the design a shot using Canva (an online graphic design platform that's incredibly easy and fast).

We've made it easy for anyone who is even slightly aesthetically-inclined to step in and handle this task for you. You can find straightforward design instructions, including templates for laying out the content and images in Canva, starting back on page 50.

Whoever does the design needs some simple instructions from you as well. But it will only take you 5-10 minutes.

They'll need to know what kind of images you like and don't like.

> If your designer is internal, we recommend a subscription to Envato Elements.
>
> The cost per month is low, and the variety and quality of images available for use in permission assets is excellent.
>
> Your designer can easily download images you identify, and images related to images you identify. So your permission asset is visually consistent throughout.
>
> If your designer is external, they likely have access to their own licensed imaging platform. You can give them examples from Envato Elements or Google or still images from videos you like on YouTube and they'll find equivalents.

Give your designer 4 days to turn the design around for their first permission asset. Once they have 1 permission asset under their design belt, they should be able to turn the design around increasingly fast. Eventually it's a 1-day task, plus a couple days for any custom Infographics you are embedding in it.

Once the designer submits your completed permission asset, spot check to make sure everything is as it should be.

- Is there a cover page that follows the templates on page 50?
- Is there an index/table of contents?
- Does every page other than the cover have a footer with the page #, your url, and your logo or company name?
- Is your logo on the cover of the permission asset?
- Are the links in the permission asset formatted correctly (blue text, underlined)?
- *Does anything look weird?*

If it passes your test, it will pass every prospect's test too.

And with that, you have officially conducted the creation of your first thought leadership permission asset.

Congratulations!

Remember, thought leadership is a double threat. It's going to generate leads directly as prospects download it, love it, and choose to work with you because of it.

But it also has a mystical effect. You'll talk about it with potential partners at trade shows. You'll run workshops on it. You'll speak on podcasts about it. And by being visible and interesting, you generate interest in your business. You become an asset. A driver of revenue.

The book you're reading right now is, boiled down, a thought leadership permission asset.

We chose this format because it's powerful, and it looks like you feel the same.

So let's start working on the next phase of your journey.

What do you do next? Skip to page 73 to learn about the landing page and more.

Chapter 6

INSTANTLY INSPIRE CONFIDENCE AND TRUST IN YOUR PROSPECTS.

Permission asset type #2. **Case study.**

Another type of permission asset is a case study. We generally recommend case studies for Claire the Creator only. Why? Because it involves time spent talking with customers and thinking deeply about the most valuable ideas to lean into. That's best suited for a Creator with time to spend on it, not Conductors or Curators with other duties.

The idea with a case study is to reflect a story your prospect can relate to.

Show them you:

- Solved a problem like theirs

- Solved a unique challenge and you're capable of solving theirs.

But wait. None of my customers want to talk after they get what they want!

Ain't that the truth. In B2B it's particularly tough getting a customer to chat after the transaction is complete.

Sometimes you're lucky enough to get a pre-chat, and that fizzles out. Most of the time you get ghosted.

However! There are some tricks you can use to make that interview more likely (trick #1 being *don't call it an interview*).

- Ask! As the last step in the sales process, get your sales rep to simply ask the customer if you can contact them in a few weeks. "Can we reach back out for a quick follow up chat to see how everything's going and get some feedback on your experience?"

- Bribe! "We like to get case studies from our favorite customers, and anyone who participates gets a $100 Amazon gift card. Would you like one?"

- Follow up! Put together a simple email automation that follows up with every customer. "We enjoyed working with you and would like to slot in a quick chat to gather feedback on how your particle counters are working out. You can book it in my schedule at this link, or just let me know when it works best for you and I'll block that time and give you a call."

So many opportunities are missed because we just don't ask. People want to talk about themselves, and you're giving them the chance.

A unique angle on your case study is always better, in our experience, than something universal. There's an argument for a case study addressing a very common application, but usually readers are drawn to something unique.

Something about their own industry that makes them laugh or learn or nod in agreement. **Something that makes them feel validated** in some way. Like a parent scrolling through Instagram and stopping on a video about getting their kids buckled into the car seat. *I totally get that. It's hard and it sucks. This makes me feel good and validated. I better subscribe to this for more!*

Something that shows them a flicker of their own challenge, and they'll fill in the gaps so they see themselves.

Seems like a tall order, but all it takes is a little time sitting at your computer with a blank document on the screen ready to type out ideas. Brainstorm, like you did in highschool, and you'll find the inspiration you need.

Next, starting on page 66, you'll find some specific info on how to write a case study.

How do you actually write a case study?

Everyone thinks they can write a case study.

It's easy, just write about what happened!

Then they write it and it sucks. Because it's not just about what happened. It's about why. And telling the story of why in a compelling way.

The *why* is the old world marinara sauce. Without it, even the freshest noodles (or the best possible what) are tough to swallow.

So here's the simple process to make that compelling narrative create itself.

Step 1. Interviews!

You can certainly write a case study with a few emails back and forth. But that has a high likelihood of turning into one of those noodles with no sauce things.

The best thing you can do is talk to these people:

- The person who bought the thing

- The person who helped the person buy the thing.

- The person who is using the thing now (if different from the person who bought - graduate students using an apparatus purchased by a principal investigator in a university lab, for example)

In the best case scenario you talk to each of them twice.

In the second-best case scenario, you talk to each twice and get some follow up questions answered through email.

In the third-best case scenario, you talk once, but you get plenty of information to build the case study in that single conversation.

But what kind of things do I ask in those conversations? I'm no journalist!

Take a note from your kids. Or your niece and nephew. Or the annoying kid next door.

You can ask why in a hundred different ways!

Why did you choose us over the other brand?

Why did you need a new solution in the first place?

Why was this a good solution?

Why did you choose this model over another model we offer?

Why did you decide to call us vs. completing a form on the website?

Why **didn't** you choose **this competing solution**?

Why didn't this seem like a risky purchase to you?

Why did you need this **now**?

Why are you changing the way you do X?

Why AREN'T you changing the way you do X?

Why is this the right use of your budget?

Why can't you do this with existing tools in your workplace?

Of course you should ask the *what* questions too:

What were you using before this?

What made this the right solution?

What prompted you to contact us on the day?

What does your application look like now?

What was the problem before?

What else could you have done with this budget?

What could we have done differently?

What did we do right?

What improvement has this made to your everyday?

What is the long term impact of this purchase to your work?

What's the most immediate impact to your work?

What kind of research did you do before contacting us?

A lot of the what questions are reframings of the *why* questions. That's sort of the point. You'll dig up more valuable insights by reframing questions.

Step 2. Start writing

There are a few different ways to start writing your case study. We all have different styles. And some of us haven't discovered our style yet. So here are a few different ways you could start.

Try writing like you're making an infographic.

This is handy because later, you can make your case study into an infographic. We'll talk more about this below.

Here's the easiest way to organize your thoughts to start writing like an infographic.

1. Who is the customer?

2. What was their challenge?

3. What did they need to overcome that challenge?

4. How did you (or your colleague) approach the challenge?

5. What was the identified solution?

6. What were the results for the customer?

An infographic has to be concise and orderly, so organizing your thoughts as though you're making an infographic can help.

Check out these infographics as an example. Orderly, clear, compelling*
www.jbbgi.com/infographic

Try writing it like a story.

Even if you haven't written a story before, you've read them. You watch movies.

So start at the beginning.

1. What is the setting?
    On a swampy patch of land in the south of Florida is unassuming white, sterile building filled with the brightest minds in your industry…

2. What is happening?
    They're working out ways to build a better rainbow-colored ketchup manufacturing line…

3. And what's the problem?
    But getting the yellow ketchup to stop bleeding into the green is a huge problem…

You successfully set the stage for a story to unfold. Where your business helps this beleaguered soul overcome a challenge and achieve success (whether that's profits or any other landmark achievement to that customer).

Try writing it like an interview.

When you interview the customer, you ask your questions in an organized order. One thing naturally leads to the next.

So you already did most of the work.

If you don't feel your customers need all the razmataz of a story or a refined presentation, give them the interview.

Or try writing it like a thought leadership piece.

We outlined detailed steps to walk through when creating thought leadership content starting on page 40.

It starts with the mind map. And the positioning of your problem or solution in the middle of the mind map.

This works just as well for a case study.

In fact, you could create your mind map before you do your interview. Or after your first interview, but before your follow up interview.

You can use it however you feel comfortable. It's going to be a big help.

Step 3. The visuals

A case study is most effective when it comes with interesting visuals.

A lot of B2B manufacturers or distributors don't consider the design elements that most prospects are actually very drawn to.

But your prospects are people. People like pictures and colors. Neglecting the visual element of your case study can waste all the time and energy that went into getting the interviews, researching, doing them, and spinning it all into words that matter.

If there are field applications for the case study subject in question (like our example above) field imagery is always compelling.

If there is historical information about the subject of the case study, historical images are super cool.

This image is way more interesting

Than this image

If you started writing your case study with the infographic method, you can easily create an infographic to go along with it.

Then you can use that infographic on social media, in emails. You can print it and bring it to tradeshows. You can drop it from an airplane as you fly over the workplace of your ideal customer. You can turn it into a billboard and plaster it along every major commuter route across your most valuable service area.

Step 4. The review

The last step is to do an honest review before you let this permission asset loose on the world.

Of course you want prospects to download this so you capture their information. But you don't want them to download it, read it, and dismiss your brand based on what they read.

You don't want them to feel bamboozled. You want them to see value. So they continue with the relationship and take a step forward with your business.

Don't forget, your prospects aren't solopreneurs. They are surrounded by other influencers inside their organizations. Stakeholders in the acquisition of this new asset you're trying to sell.

You want them to quote your permission asset. Screenshot it. Put it in their budget request proposals and internal powerpoint presentations. **You want them to easily arm themselves with information so they can convince their bosses to allocate budget with no resistance.**

The word count rule of thumb!

Your case study should be at least 1,500 words long.

Anything less and the story might not be interesting enough to tell. Or you're leaving out important/valuable details.

On the other end, 3,500 words is about as much length as you can expect a reader to endure.

Too short and the reader could feel tricked into download a blog post without any deep insights into their issue.

Too long and the reader will skim, missing important points that could have turned them into a customer.

Chapter 7

SAVE YOUR PROSPECTS TIME AND ENERGY TO WIN THE SALE.

Permission asset type #3. **Buying guide.**

The last type of permission asset we recommend is the buying guide. The humble buying guide.

But we don't recommend it 3rd because it's less-than the others. It's a great permission asset because it solves a problem the prospect has the moment they have it.

They're looking at a product category or a product on your website and:

- They aren't sure the product does what they need.
- They aren't sure what they need to begin with.
- They aren't sure the comparative value of your product vs. other brands (not the literal dollar value, but the value-for-budget).
- They aren't sure what's marketing spin and what's real.
- They aren't sure what's changed since the last time they spent budget on this kind of product.
- They aren't sure how to narrow down their choices.
- They aren't sure how trustworthy your brand is.

So with a buying guide, you can calm a ton of uncertainty at a critical point in the buying process.

Probably THE most critical point. Because **the buying guide appeals to the best kind of lead you can get.** These prospects are ready to buy right now. They're <u>actively trying to figure out what to buy.</u>

So with the buying guide you:

1. Gain their trust.

2. Nudge them toward your product.

3. Build some loyalty to your brand.

But most B2Bs have the wrong idea about buying guides.

They incorrectly assume the prospect landing on the website has already decided to buy from them. So they make product guides, or product line guides, instead of high level buying guides.

And those product guides almost always (also) make assumptions about the reader - like the reader is familiar with the latest jargon and technology, or uses the product for the most common application. Even an experienced lab manager may not have purchased the equipment type you sell before. The one in their lab has worked fine for 10 years. They use it every day, but they don't know what the options are outside the model they use every morning.

Think of the laser printer in your office. You bought it 5 or 7 years ago. It worked great. But last week it started jamming. So you need a replacement. You know you want duplex printing, and legal size sheet feed - that's what your current model has.

But you don't know a whole lot about cloud printing or dedicated mobile apps that accompany printers. They weren't around the last time you were in the market. Even though you print stacks of pages every day, you still need a quick briefing on which of these new features might be a benefit to your everyday work.

So when you make assumptions about your customers you lose opportunities. Sales. Profits.

Here's the easiest way to characterize the difference between a product guide and a buying guide.

Product guide	**Buying guide**
Here are the differences between our products.	Here's how you shop for the best value in this product category from any manufacturer.

That's not to say you shouldn't have product guides. But...

- Buying guides appeal to people who are in-market right now. They're actively looking to purchase, and it's the most direct way to get them to reveal themselves AND nudge them toward your products.

- A buying guide is among the 20% of tactics that will drive 80% of your results.

- A buying guide can subtly do the same things as a product guide, but without the overt self promotion and associated annoyance from prospects.

A buying guide should be your priority because it appeals to the largest group of your prospects. **And they're ready to buy right now.** We can't say that enough. That's like the 3rd time we said it in 5 pages.

It's the highest quality lead you can get. And you're solving a challenge of theirs at the most critical point.

Nobody in the history of life on Earth has downloaded a buying guide about a metalworking lathe or an incubator for fun. They download it becuase they want to buy a metalworking lathe or an incubator.

And whether you're a Claire. Chris, or Charles you can create it, or direct the creation of it, in-house and with very little effort.

How do you actually write a buying guide?

That depends on who you are.

Conductors, Curators, Creators - everybody starts at the same place.

You choose the product category that needs the guide most urgently.

But you each do it in a different way (you can try using the other streams' methods, but this book is here to help you do everything as efficiently as possible. The methods identified for you below are, in our opinions, the easiest, most accurate, and most valuable).

There's a bit of subjectivity in it. Sometimes your boss or your boss' boss says you need to sell more of a particular product. The brand has poured a lot of money into developing a new product and needs to get every bit of momentum it can.

Sometimes you're just doing your job. You want to increase sales because you want to take home more profits (because you're the boss) or you want to ask for a big raise (because you're employed).

So here's how each of you find the right subject for your buying guide and how you get it made.

Claire the Creator - look at Google Analytics

The best starting point for Creators is in Google Analytics. This is good for two reasons.

1. It helps you find the target for the guide, which will increase the number of high-value leads you capture. It easily and qualifiably tells you what people are interested in. And that's the main thing you're trying to do right now.

2. It gives you insights into parts of the website that aren't converting. And you can plan to fix those parts of the website over the next 6 months, making yourself more valuable to the business, securing your role, making a good case for a pay increase. (For more on conversion rate optimization - because you DO want all that, right?!?! That's what this book is for - go to page 153)

So what do you look at for insights about the buying guide you should write?

*   Look at product pages with most views (do these already have buying guides? If not, the guide will increase the success of these pages).
*   Look at category pages with the most views (same as above).
*   Look at the pages with the longest time on page (people are engaged with this product and willing to spend more time learning).

Armed with your data, the choice is yours.

And once you've settled on your buying guide subject, it's time to plan, research, and write.

How Claire the Creator should write a buying guide.

Open up your Google doc and write this line at the very top, in H1 sizing so it's always easy to go back to and remember.

The buying guide is built around this statement - **Here's how you shop for the best value in this product category from any manufacturer.**

After you have your Google doc prepared with that line, grab a piece of paper and get ready for your mind map .

We talked a bit about the mind map in the thought leadership section (page 44). And you can go back for a bit more if you want a refresher.

But if you want to get to the doing, here's how:

1. Write the product or product category in a circle in the middle of the page (this circle is called a node).

2. Write a feature from your product page (the flagship product in your chosen product category) in a node somewhere around the central node.

3. Surround your features node with other nodes like:

    a.   Why does this feature matter?

    b.   What does this feature do?

    c.   What is the main benefit of this feature?

    d.   What are other benefits?

    e.   What alternatives serve a similar purpose?

    f.   How does this feature compare to alternative features?

    g.   What were older versions of this feature like?

    h.   What happens without this feature?

    i.   What applications are particularly well-enabled by this feature?

    j.   How does this feature relate to other features?

k. How does this benefit the user's daily work?

l. How does this impact the upfront cost of the product?

m. How does this impact the long term cost of ownership of the product?

n. Who does this feature benefit most? Who can do without it?

o. Scenarios where this feature saved the day.

p. Scenarios where this feature wasn't present, and the consequences.

4. Complete this for every feature in your chosen product category, and more if there are common features in the category which your product doesn't incorporate.

You don't have to answer all the questions from A-P. And there are probably questions specific to your industry we haven't included.

The point of this, though, is more questions answered result in a more comprehensive buying guide. And **a more comprehensive buying guide results** in more leads and, what your boss wants, **more revenue.**

9 out of 10 Creators will look at the mind map and say *I don't have the answers to all these questions. What the hell!*

And that's alright. Because there are people in the business with the answers. You just have to book a time to chat through this with them.

We recommend:

| Senior sales staff. | An application or product engineer in the business. | Your boss. |

Before your chat, format your Google doc further.

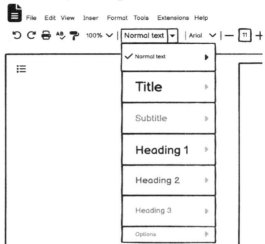

Title: The center bubble of your mind map.
Heading 2: Use these throughout your doc - these are all the features you listed in your mind map.
Normal text: All the questions you intend to answer under each heading 2.

With the document formatted like this, it will be quick and easy for you to get all the information you need to complete your buying guide permission asset.

When you sit down for your chat with that senior sales rep, bring your laptop with your Google doc open and walk through your questions under each feature heading. And once you're done chatting, you have the content for your buying guide in organized sections. All you have to do at this point is some formatting and design.

If there isn't anyone in the business to help you find the answers to these questions, you'll have to do your research online. And you can find info on where and how to look in the Curator section on the next few pages or the section on Reddit, YouTube, LinkedIn, and Google on page 52.

Designing your buying guide.

Designing your buying guide is just like designing your thought leadership or case study permission assets.

There are step-by-step instructions, including guides to follow when you create your design, back on page 50.

The only difference is that your buying guide should, if possible, contain more pictures of the product (ideally in action) than the thought leadership permission asset discussed earlier in the book.

When your design is complete, you're ready to move on to page 88.

Chris the Curator - look at your sales data

Existing sales data is an easy source of key metrics you can use to pick your buying guide target. And it's most accessible and familiar to Curators (Charles the Conductor as well, but this section isn't for you) because you regularly talk with colleagues about it, talk to customers about it, think about it, plan around it.

To find the most appropriate target based on sales data, look for:

- Largest sales volume
- Largest gross margin-dollars products
- Largest opportunity for growth - sales aren't currently explosive but you know your competitors are having challenges fulfilling orders, for example.
- Longest sales cycle, so you can shorten the sales cycle

The data is all in your CRM, or in your brain.

When the target is chosen, you can start curating the content for it.

How Chris the Curator should produce the buying guide.

You are trying to get this done with as little time and effort as possible.

Depending on your experience in the business, and with this product category, there are two ways to do it.

Both start with a mind map. You can follow the same guidelines we gave your Creator colleagues at the start of this chapter.

Then, the first way is to find the relevant content posted all over the Internet and curate it. So your prospects can get something comprehensive from you that would require them reading many different sources over the course of hours or days.

To do that, you can follow the steps outlined in the earlier chapter on thought leadership permission assets, with one significant difference. You're going to start by searching on Google first (so that's #4 on the earlier list). And you'll work your way backwards through the other sources (3, then 2, then 1).

The nature of the buying guide means you might not have to do anything other than search on Google. Starting there could save you tons of time and effort.

So you have a completed mind map, and you're going to use Google (first) to answer as many questions in the nodes your mind map branches out to as possible.

For an example of what this will generally what it will look visit **www.jbbgi.com/mindmap**

Paste your curated answers under each question heading.

When each is complete, or as many as you feel comfortable with, paste each section individually into ChatGPT with the following prompt:

You are an expert in the field of XYZ. Your job is to rewrite the entire text below with conversational language assuming the reader has a limited understanding of the content. Try to engage the user with your writing. Avoid large blocks of text by formatting with ordered and unordered lists, tables and charted data. Avoid the common phrases that readers or AI content detectors would use to flag this as AI generated content. The text to rewrite is this: INSERT YOUR TEXT HERE.

The AI will do its thing and you can paste the rewritten, curated text into the space of the previous text in your Google doc. You get unique content, better than the original you sourced online, in less than 5 minutes.

That's the first way.

The second way is to simply answer the questions yourself.

If your role is heavily involved in sales or applications or product development, as many Curators are, you can probably answer most of the questions you need to (remember, they're back on page 78) without any online research.

Remember - the buying guide is meant to teach prospects about a product category. And if your primary role involves selling or something else with intimate product knowledge, you have everything you need already in your head.

You just need to put it on the page in an orderly way using the mind map above, the questions above, and the format in the Google doc above.

And when you're ready to design, flip back to page 50 and use the easy Canva design guide to get it done in a couple hours.

Here is how Charles the Conductor can write a buyers guide permission asset - Find content gaps and look inward

Here's the thing about choosing the product to feature in your buying guide as a Conductor.

You can do what we recommend for Claire the Creator or Chris the Curator over the last few pages. Or you can do either of these two things:

Look for gaps.

There are two places you could look for gaps.

On your own website and on competitor websites.

Let's start with your own website.

Do you already have buying guides on any of your product pages?

Choose one without a guide.

The end.

But that's not very strategic. So combine it with this next part.

Do your main competitors have buying guides on important product category and individual product pages? If not, prospects are being underserved and you can provide value your competitors aren't.

So your competitors don't have a buying guide and you don't also? Create one for that product category.

Or... —>

Just make a decision.

Conductors are uniquely familiar with the metabolism of the business.

You already spend a lot of time with sales and customer data. You use this data to manage the people working under you.

And you are in the position to simply make this decision.

Increasing sales of X products is my priority right now.

X is what your buying guide will focus on.

How Charles the Conductor should produce the buying guide.

There are 2 different ways to get this done, and there are 3 different things you need done.

You need a mind map for organization, you need the permission asset written, you need the permission asset designed.

To get this done:

#1 Make the mind map the first deliverable you ask for from someone else. Your sales manager. Your best sales person. Your director of business development. A long-term applications engineer. But not someone in your marketing department.

There's a template for the mind map back on page 44. But the person you give the task of creating a mind map to will likely have additional insightful questions to add.

And that's what makes them an ideal person to not only create the mind map, but to complete the written content of the permission asset.

The mind map for a buying guide permission asset is basically a series of questions about your chosen product category that need answering. That's what your buying guide permission asset is also. Answers to the questions new buyers have. Amalgamated in one place and with your brand name on it.

So you ask the sales manager for the mind map, which helps them organize their thoughts on the product category. Then you ask them to complete the questions they placed under each heading - information they already know upside down and inside out.

The mind map and the permission asset format document (available here **www.jbbgi.com/mindmap**) help keep your staff organized as they create this document.

If you don't have an in-house expert who can create content beyond the mindmap or your favorite B2B marketing agency on retainer, you could to hire a Creator on freelancer marketplaces like upwork.com

Bonus points if you find a Creator with copywriting and design skills listed on their profile, because they'll also design the PDF after you approve the content they wrote for you.

For these freelancers:

1. Send them the mind map your internal team created.
2. Send them the example formatting of the permission asset from **www.jbbgi.com/permissionasset**
3. Tell them you'll need to approve the content before they go ahead with the design.

Want to be sure you aren't getting plagiarized work from your Creator?

You don't need to subscribe to any expensive plagiarism detecting software to keep your Creator honest.

The biggest giveaways are big words and technical explanations.

So spot check your Creator's content on Google.

Copy the sentence you suspect might be plagiarized. Paste it into a plain old Google search. You'll find out very quickly where your Creator sourced their information, and how much work they put into giving you unique content (you know - what you're paying them for).

From here, it's just a matter of you approving the content they create. If you approve of the words, and you approve of the design, you can move on to the next section on page 88.

…but hear us out on this next bit.

#2 Write the buying guide yourself.

Because of your deep knowledge of the business and its products, you might be able to answer all the questions in the mind map faster yourself than it takes to assign and review work done by others.

We know you have a lot on your shoulders, and writing a buying guide doesn't necessarily seem like something you want to do.

But you might be the best person in the business to do it. And your experience means you'll probably do it 10X faster than anyone else.

There's no need for you to design it. That can go to anyone else on your team with even a little technical aptitude. Instructions for them to follow are right here on page 50.

Answer the questions in the nodes branding off the main topic of the mind map yourself. Put those answers into a copy of the template found at **www.jbbgi.com/permissionasset** , then send it to your chosen designer with the instructions we gave.

Excellent side-effect of approach #2: Everyone in the business will be reminded of your deep knowledge of the industry, products, and customers. They'll be reminded why they work for you. And how they can learn from you. It's wild to say, but this will actually contribute to staff retention and positive energy through the company or department. Staff will look at it like you're getting down in the trenches and they'll love it.

When your permission asset is designed, you can move to the next chapter.

Chapter 8

STEP # 3. EASILY CONVINCE YOUR PROSPECTS TO SHARE THEIR CONTACT INFO.

This is where so many B2B brands fall flat - and where you'll be an outlier.

Over the next few dozen pages, you'll learn how to write, design, and deploy a landing page where users are funneled to trade their contact information for your permission asset.

We're making it as easy as possible for the person creating the permission asset to repurpose existing content into the landing page. You'll see wireframes for the design, an easy checklist for the 8 elements you need on the landing page, and practical tips to make it all as low-energy and user-friendly as possible.

So without further ado…

How do prospects exchange their information for your permission asset?

The most common way is via a landing page. Or a squeeze page if you prefer. Or a chazzwazzers page. One of those is not real. Did you google it? You should.

It's a page on your website with a form (and lots more) where the user inputs their name and email to download the permission asset.

But the success of the landing page isn't guaranteed. Most permission asset landing pages convert (that is, turn a prospect into a lead) at less than 1.5%. Because most landing pages don't make a compelling case for the prospect to download the permission asset.

In this section, we're going to show you how to craft a landing page to blow that 1.5% conversion rate to smithereens. One that's full of passion, excitement, validation, benefits. **Everything your prospects want and need to go from an anonymous website user to a hot lead and, eventually, a high-lifetime-value customer.**

Here's what you need (and don't need) on your landing page:

1. No site navigation.

2. A form.

3. A strong above the fold image and heading with supporting subheading text.

4. Social proof.

   a. Social proof supporting the professional position of your business until you have social proof pertaining to the permission asset itself.

5. Excerpts of content from the permission asset.

6. Images from the permission asset.

7. Frequently asked questions.

8. Calls to action.

We'll dig a little deeper into this now.

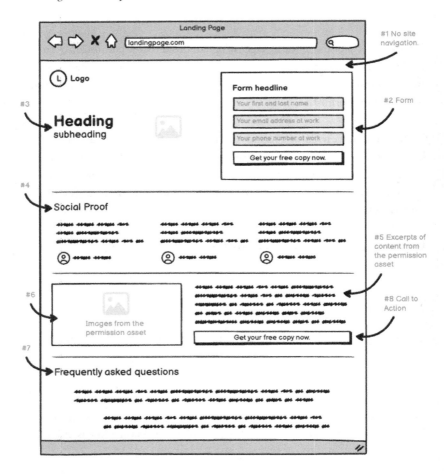

#1 Why should you hide the website navigation on your landing page?

People get distracted. People want the path of least resistance. Everything wants the path of least resistance. Ever wonder why, out of the entire forest, the bear or deer chooses to walk along the human hiking trail (or, as it turns out, the human chooses to walk along the bear or deer trail)?

Path of least resistance!

Out of necessity on your landing page you introduce an element of friction. Resistance. **The form**. The prospect has to complete the form to get the permission asset. Without the form, you don't get any information about the prospect.

In that moment, when they are on the verge of sharing their information, it's easier to click away on the site navigation than to complete the form.

So you remove website navigation to take away the temptation. In doing so, you double the number of leads you get from your landing page vs a landing page with website navigation.

#**2** **Are all forms equal, and how can I make my form awesome?**

Two elements of your landing page live above the fold. One is hero messaging (which we'll talk about below in #3). And 1 is the form.

The form usually sits above the fold, occupying the right ⅓ to ½ of the screen.

The form is the last hurdle your prospect has to overcome before giving you their information. It's the gatekeeper for all your leads. You need to get it right.

And you can!

So let's run it down real quick here.

There are 4 elements to your form.

1. The heading.
2. The form fields.

3.   The placeholder text.
4.   The button text.

The heading on most forms is overlooked, neglected - a missed opportunity. Look at the text above the form fields on your competitors' permission assets. Even their contact us forms on their product pages. It's generic and does nothing to enlighten and empower a prospect.

Your heading should be benefits focused.

Learn how your business can benefit for free.	**Get your free copy & cut your research time in half.**	**See how to improve XYZ today!**

It doesn't take much to make your form heading more appealing. And it pays off in leads.

The form fields and placeholder text for a permission asset form should be minimal.

Each field on your form is a point of friction. The more you ask, the less likely a prospect is to complete the form.

The permission asset itself already gives you a lot of information about the prospect.

- The type of product or service they're in market for.
- Their willingness to engage in education.
- Their openness to your brand.

And a few simple fields in your form give you any other information you need:

- To target them with follow up marketing.
- For your sales team to meaningfully follow up with.

Generally, here's what we recommend for most B2B permission asset forms.

Name:	Your first and last name
Email Address:	Your email address at work
Phone #:	Your phone number at work

You could even make the phone # non compulsory. Or leave it out entirely. But we like it and have had success collecting phone contact information for our clients over the last 10-12 years.

The button text should never be the default text set by your form builder.

> **Submit**

...not very compelling text.

> **Download**

...downloads sound like they take a long time, big commitment. So avoid that too.

You want to keep reinforcing the value the prospect gets by downloading the permission asset.

> **Get your free copy now.**

> **Make my job easier!**

> **I'm ready to learn.**

#3 Your above-the-fold text and imagery.

The image and copy above the fold sharing this coveted space with your form are your most valuable assets on this page.

They set the prospects' expectations. And build their excitement. And push them past the friction that comes with filling in any form online.

The **image** needs to match the prospect's expectation. Don't lead with a hero image set in a tropical rainforest if your permission asset is a thought leadership piece on product applications in the arctic.

But also don't feel too constrained by the B2B-ness of things. You still sell to people, and people like quirky, creative things.

We once wrote a thought leadership piece for a client manufacturing biological safety cabinets. And the hero image contained a handful of BSC's involved in a prison break. It was awesome.

But the image doesn't have to be quirky. Sometimes it makes more sense to show your prospects something familiar. Something they can relate to. A scene they see themselves in - as long as it's related to the subject matter in your permission asset.

Where can you find inspiration for this imagery?

You may already have some great ideas for engaging imagery in your permission asset. You could expand one of those into above the fold imagery. You could spend some time on YouTube exploring videos related to your permission asset's subject matter. You could look at your competitors' websites. You could look at the images Google returns when you search there.

The text should be short but impactful. It needs to fill in the spaces the image can't.

Not the physical spaces on the screen. The logical spaces in your prospect's understanding.

There is space here for a heading and a subheading.
The heading is your main message, the subheading supports that message.

The heading is short. The subheading is less short.

And you can probably place your text in one of two camps.

1.   Something controversial.
2.   Something beneficial.

If your permission asset is a piece of thought leadership, you might have something controversial to say. And that's what brought prospects here in the first place. So lay it out there.

If your permission asset is a buying guide or case study, it probably lends itself more to a statement of benefit to the prospect. What will the reader get out of this permission asset? You wrote it with purpose, so boil that purpose down to its essence.

#**4** Social proof to put prospects at ease.

Whether we admit it to ourselves or not, we're all influenced by our peers.

Maybe it's because we don't want to feel like suckers alone. **Maybe it's because we all feel like imposters,** but trust others to help us stay on the right path. Maybe it doesn't matter.

When we see a peer has received some benefit from a business, we get a little more comfortable with that business. We give a little trust.

And your permission asset landing page is the place to build that trust with social proof.

Social proof = testimonials

Yes, it's just a fancy rebranding of old-news testimonials. But they work. So use them!

How do I use social proof when my permission asset is brand new?

Great question!

You have to get creative in the start. But you're used to that.

The social proof doesn't have to be explicitly about your permission asset. You just have to find some positive words about your business with a tenuous connection to the content in your permission asset.

So...

1. Look on Google for "YOUR BUSINESS NAME or YOUR PRODUCT NAME reviews".

2. Visit Reddit and type your business name or product names into the search bar and see what people are saying.

3. Rinse and repeat with other social networks (don't avoid TikTok, even if it's not quite your demographic. You'll be surprised what you learn about your customers there).

The first thing you can do is take any words you find and put them on your landing page as-is. You don't need to attribute them to anyone. They're in the public domain. But if you want to, you can do one of two things.

1. You can attribute it to the user and the social media platform in a few ways. If it's a platform like Reddit where users have aliases (MuscleArms1982, for example), you can attribute it to the alias. We don't do this, but there's no reason you can't. If it's a platform where every user is "real", like Facebook or LinkedIn, you can attribute it to John B. on LinkedIn.

2. Or you can contact the person who said the thing about your business and ask them for permission to post it with their name and business. Or you can ask them for a different testimonial altogether. Every one of these social platforms has direct messaging you can use to start that conversation.

When you start getting more permission asset downloads from this landing page, you can use the contact information you collect to solicit more specific social proof about the permission asset itself. Obviously, this is more valuable on the landing page than the general social proof in #1 and #2 above.

Email prospects two days after they download the permission asset. Ask what they thought. And if their response is favorable, ask if you could publish their thoughts on your landing page.

Example email to send to prospects you want permission asset testimonials from.

Hi firstname (*note - it's best to use the first name. But if you don't have the first name for some reason, insert any cordial greeting).

Hope your week is going great so far. I heard that Phoenix commute can be rough in the summer.

My name's John and I work at XYZ company. I actually wrote the buying guide you downloaded the other day on mercury analyzers.

I'm trying to make it as valuable as possible to people like yourself. Could you help your peers get more value from it by providing a little feedback? Just two questions.

1.   Did you get any useful insights from the guide?
2.   Was there anything you hoped to learn but found missing from the guide?

I'll incorporate your feedback into the guide immediately so the next person to download gets more of the good stuff they need.

I'd also love to help you with anything you need related to our mercury analyzers. If you want a product demo or validation documents for your application, I can do that.

Just let me know.

Thanks!
John

The rule of thumb is to have three pieces of social proof on your landing page. All of them together in a row.

If you can get pictures of the social proofers, great! If they're willing to share their workplace, job title, or any other information that makes them (and you) seem more trustworthy to your prospects, great!

Social proof usually lives somewhere in the middle of your landing page. Below the fold, but not at the bottom of the page. It's too valuable to be at the bottom of the page. Most people never get past the first scroll of the mouse wheel on a page.

#5 Landing page element - Excerpts of content from the permission asset to give users a taste of the value they'll get from it.

You might have kids. You were, at one point (maybe long, long ago) a kid yourself. And in the toy store, where kids dreams come true, there are toys with colorful, inviting packaging. And the most inviting part of all, the hole in the plastic or cardboard with the enlightened words "try me".

Oh the sound of Buzz Lightyear's sage advice. Barbie *asking do you want to have a pizza party?* The robotic clang of Optimus Prime transforming.

The sneak peak is not just for physical products. They're for knowledge products as well. Your permission asset is no exception.

You can give the prospect a little sample of your permission asset on this landing page.

How do you do it?

Take your most impactful 2-3 sentences. Or your most provocative. Or your most empowering. Pair them with an image from your permission asset, and place it below the midpoint of your landing page.

Anyone who scrolls this far is searching for something to push them over the edge. They weren't totally hooked by your hero image and form.

The social proof wasn't what they needed.

Maybe what they need is a little taste of the value they'll get by exchanging their contact information for your permission asset.

So place that content somewhere around here:

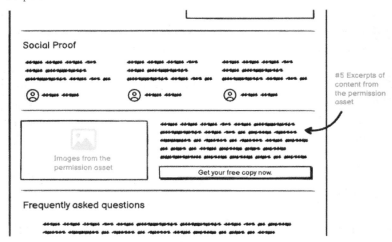

#5 Excerpts of content from the permission asset

#6 Images you made, or had made, or used, for the permission asset should be used on your landing page too.

Creative energy went into the images in your permission asset. They conjure the feel you want your prospects to get from the content in the PDF file you designed.

Don't trap the output of that creative energy in chains. Let it free! Share it with the world.

Support the words on your landing page with your best permission asset images.

If they show the application - awesome.

If they're creative and funny - awesome.

If they're generic and boring (sometimes you only have the images you have) - it's alright. You can always improve these over time as you find new sources (but have you looked at the places we recommend on **www.jbbgi.com/resources**?)

The point is - a landing page is visual, and you already have great visuals in your permission asset. So use them!

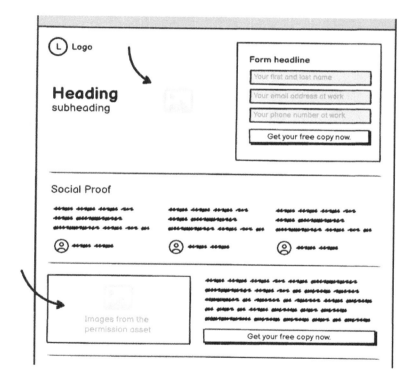

#7 Frequently asked questions can help calm prospects' worries.

You already know the questions your prospects are going to ask. You tried to answer them all in your permission asset. You thought deeply about them when you were planning your permission asset.

Near the bottom of your landing page, as a sort of last resort for anyone who miraculously scrolled this far, speak directly about these eight questions.

What exactly will I learn?

How will this permission asset help me in my job?

How often is this permission asset updated?

Will this help me improve my standard operating procedures or application in general?

What makes company XYZ qualified to teach me about this?

How long will this take me to read?

Who wrote this?

Who is this for?

A frequently asked questions section on your landing page makes the page as a whole more complete. You address the concerns of a certain type of prospect. One that's weary and untrusting, but interested enough to give you a chance.

They're just looking for something personal that helps them overcome their mistrust.

Of course we don't know if the FAQs will do this. But they could. And it's your job to do everything you can to get more prospects downloading this permission asset.

#8 **Calls to action that remind the prospect why they're there in the first place.**

Your landing page is built around a single action. Getting the user to exchange their information for the permission asset.

The prospects who scroll down past the hero section and away from the form need a quick and easy way to complete the transaction on the page.

It sounds wacky, but scrolling back to the top of the landing page manually is enough friction to stop some users from converting. So **each section of the page should have a button and call to action text that anchors back to the top of the page** where the prospect can complete the form.

Here are three call to action tips:

- Write short, snappy CTAs that are benefits or action focused.
- Don't ask the prospect to download the permission asset.
- Ask the prospect to learn more, to find out how, to improve their application, to save time.

Not sure how to create an anchor link for your CTA buttons? It's super easy.

1. Highlight the text in the heading of your form.
2. Right click the highlighted text.
3. Click "Copy link to highlight".
4. You now have an anchor link saved on your clipboard.
5. Paste the copied text into a Google doc so you don't lose it.

What can <u>Conductors</u> do to get this landing page done properly?

There's a landing page checklist at **www.jbbgi.com/landingpages**

Include that when you assign this permission asset work to your internal or external Claire the Creator.

You don't need to know the ins and outs of why. But you need to know everything that's supposed to get done is done.

The best person to write your landing page content is the same person writing your permission asset. And batching the work together with one person in one assignment gets it done more efficiently than any other way.

So use the checklists from this book. Assign everything at once with tons of detail (so there are no excuses later that your Creator didn't know X, Y, or Z). And verify (using the checklists) that everything you asked your Creator for is done to the letter.

What can Curators do to get this landing page done properly?

Landing page building tools can help you get the job done in less than an hour.

In a somewhat specific order, we recommend:

- Unbounce

  o Has been around forever, and is widely used. Not the best choice for beginners, but powerful for users with some experience (or time to learn).

- Leadpages

  o More templates than most other tools, fast load times, low initial cost.

- Hubspot

  - You might already use HubSpot for other parts of your day-to-day. It's landing page builder is comprehensive, and easier than Unbounce for many users.

- Odoo

  - Odoo's drag and drop landing page builder is simple and fast, with modules that fit together seamlessly. The cost is also low.

So, choose your landing page builder.

- Using the text from your permission asset, the images you chose for the design of your permission asset on Canva, and your new landing page builder, you will be able to build a high converting landing page tomorrow morning.

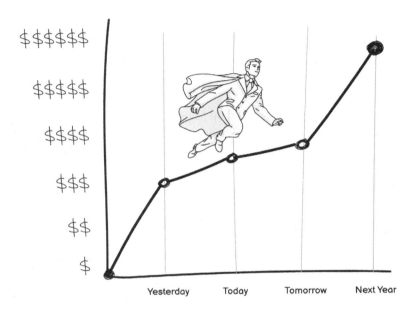

$$\$\$\$\$\$$

$$\$\$\$\$$

$$\$\$\$$

$$\$\$\$$

$$\$\$$

$$\$$

| Yesterday | Today | Tomorrow | Next Year |

Chapter 9

STEP # 4. INCREASE THE VALUE OF EVERY MARKETING ASSET YOU OR YOUR STAFF CREATE.

This is how you collect maximum leads and maximum revenue.

You're now the proud owner of some great content your prospects want to get their hands on, whether it's a thought leadership piece, a case study, or a buying guide.

And you built a killer landing page that will help prospects convert to revenue-generating lifetime customers.

But your permission asset won't achieve its destiny if left alone to fend for itself. Or help you achieve yours. It needs your help, so it can grow up to take care of you.

Which is all a fanciful way of saying you **don't just publish your landing page on your website and hope for the best.**

In the next section, we're going to show you how to **repurpose your permission asset to get maximum value.**

We're talking:

- Turning it into a blog (go to page 108).

- Turning it into emails (go to page 113).

- Promoting it with emails (go to page 115).

- Turning it into social media posts (go to page 135).

- Promoting it on social media (go to page 137).

- Turning it into a YouTube video (go to page 140).

And by maximum value, we mean it will work tirelessly for long hours to **make your job easier.** It will **generate more leads. Profits.** Turn website visitors into customers for life. Draw in prospects that never would have found you or chosen to spend budget with you in the first place.

Here's how you turn it into a super-asset that generates value for your business for years.

Chapter 10

BRING A TON MORE ORGANIC PROSPECTS TO YOUR WEBSITE FOR THE NEXT 5 YEARS.

Creators, Curators, Conductors - this should be the first thing you all do once the permission asset is complete, the landing page live, and you're ready to start collecting more leads and more revenue.

It is indeed the easiest thing you can do with your awesome, super engaging, incredibly insightful content.

Claire the Creator. Do it yourself.

Chris the Curator. Assign this to your web developer or agency.

Charles the Conductor. Assign this to your in-house Creator, your agency, or your web developer.

Why would I post this whole permission asset as a blog?

Because you limit the reach and value your content can generate by locking it behind a form on your website. And there's no reason to do that.

But if it's available freely on my website, why would anybody give me their info to download it?

Do you scour every corner of a website before you purchase or request a quote?

Chances are nobody who sees your content on the blog is going to download it from the product or category page. The same goes for anybody who downloads the permission asset.

And if someone does, they don't care. Would you? B2Bs sometimes have a tendency to overanalyze the psychology of the prospect. We all have a tendency to find problems where there aren't any. This is one of those situations.

Collect leads with your permission asset by putting it behind a form. And give your permission asset away freely. You'll attract leads and make sales via both. YOU CAN HAVE YOUR CAKE AND EAT IT TOO!

Bonus benefit

Putting the permission asset on your website as a blog (or blogs) will work some SEO magic and bring more people to your website.

How do you put your permission asset on your website as a blog? The two trains!

There are two trains of thoughts around how to optimize permission asset content on your blog.

Train #1 - Blaine the Train

The first one, the Blaine approach, is to create one single monster blog article. It's best if your content is around 1,500-3,000 words.

In most cases this is what you'll do whether you're a **Chris** or **Claire** (and what you'll ask your staff to do if you're **Charles**). It's fast and easy.

You take the entire content of the permission asset and get it on your blog.

That means...

At the very top of the blog article lives a table of contents. Every item in the table of contents hyperlinks to an anchor link further down the page.

Not sure how to create anchor links? Highlight the text further down the page you want to link to, right click, copy link to text, and you now have your anchor link.

The rest of the blog looks exactly like your permission asset (use the same pictures, headings, font, formatting, all of it) with one significant difference. In every section or two, you insert a call to action in the text or in a button that asks the reader if they want to download the full version of the content.

That call to action links to your awesome squeeze page. The prospect becomes an awesome lead. And you've done some awesome work.

In our experience, about 10% of prospects will abandon the blog, give you their contact information, and continue reading the PDF right where they left off on the blog. So if only 100 people visit your blog in the first 6 months it's posted, that's still 10 leads you would have missed before.

What's the value of 10 leads to your business?

Train #2 - Thomas the Train

The second way, the Thomas approach, is also called the hub-and-spoke model.

It's a good choice if your content is over 4,000 words and you're a **Creator** with experience doing more detailed keyword analysis.

The hub-and-spoke model uses separate blog pages, each focused on a very targeted chapter or segment of your permission asset that on its own has search volume, pointing back to a central summary sort of blog.

We aren't writing this book to teach you how to do keyword research, but if you use Ahrefs, Moz, or Semrush, this hub-and-spoke model might be worth your time.

Here's an example of the hub in the hub-and-spoke model:

- Your permission asset is about certified reference standards.

- It has a dozen different headings (or chapters, if you prefer) throughout.

- **In your hub blog post**, you expand on the intro section of your permission asset.

  o Maybe you add some opinions or some sort of data you didn't include in the permission asset.

- **In your hub blog post,** you summarize your permission asset and each section.

  o If a section was 500 words, you summarize it in 70 or less.

- Then in each summary section you link out to the "spoke", the full content of a chosen section of the permission asset **posted as its own blog.**

Here's an example of <u>a spoke</u> in the hub-and-spoke model:

- Your permission asset is about new commercial-scale electric collators.

- One of the chapters or heading sections in your permission asset is about 12-station collators vs. 24-station collators.

- You know there's search volume because you checked in your keyword tool.

- So you take the content from that section of your permission asset and post it as a blog - even if it's 300 or 400 words.

- And here's the key part - in this blog, **you only link back to the hub blog.** This way you're sending signals to the search engines that your hub blog article is the most significant piece of this web of interconnected content.

Probably the most potent superpower of hub-and-spoke is its ability to dominate a specific competitive keyword with the hub piece of content and smaller, long-tail, high-intent keywords with the spokes.

That's all you have to do for your blog.

The most important thing is getting the permission asset content on a page on your website. If the specifics of Blaine or Thomas are intimidating, start just by getting the blog posted however you can.

That way, you can move on to some of the other fun stuff.

Chapter 11

EXPLODE THE LIFETIME VALUE OF EVERY CUSTOMER.

In the section below, we're going to explain how to use this content to **get more value from your already-most-valuable-audience.**

Your email audience is something you own. It can never be taken away.

Facebook will collapse one day. Google will disappear or take over the planet. YouTube will ban you because you used the wrong password too many times (it won't, but you get the idea). These things can be taken away from you.

Your email audience can not.

You should be doing everything you can to nurture it, feed it, give it good things so it gives you good things in return.

Your permission asset is an amazing thing you created. And the people who will be most impressed by it are already in your contact list.

There are other reasons you want to use your permission asset content in email marketing. And we're going to list some of them here.

1. You want people to click on the link in the email to go to the website so they can explore more of what you have to offer that's both related and unrelated to the permission asset itself (this is a given).

2. You want to pixel them with remarketing tags (more on this later on page 190).

3. You want them to visit other blog articles so they're impressed with your expertise and your commitment to your customers.

4. You want them to view a product detail page or services detail page they wouldn't have found otherwise, and for that to imprint on their mind so they come back when they're in-market.

5. You want them to spark a memory around something they've been procrastinating, and book an appointment with you on a real time availability calendar to solve that problem.

6. You want them to raise their hand and identify what most interests them about the email they received. For example, if you are in the unfortunate situation of marketing to a unsegmented list and an email you send presents options for three different market segments, they could click on their segment so future emails can be targeted specifically to them. Being more specific in your emails will be part of your long-term strategy.

7. You want your email audience to see the value in your brand by giving away useful information for free.

8. You want them to think of you first, because they've recently seen you in their inbox, when they need something.

9. You want them to let you know they're in-market, so you can **capture more revenue from them.**

The point is, you should be communicating with your email audience more, and your permission asset is the perfect kind of value to share with them. It's an actual win-win for both parties to share valuable information (you - the permission asset. Them - their problem) and help each others businesses thrive.

And to do that, you're going to send 7 emails over the next 3 months.

<u>Claire the Creator,</u> here's what you do next.

You have your goals in mind.

You have the content you created fresh in your mind (after all, you poured all your energy and creativity into this permission asset and you're an expert on all the angles it covers).

Now you are going to plan how it will roll out to your email audience.

Remember, you're going to send 7 emails over the next 3(ish) months.

And you're going to write emails that use your permission asset content, tease your permission asset content, and compel readers with content they're drawn to.

Here's what we know for sure, and how it plays into your planning.

People engage with content in different ways.

- Some are analytical.
- Some are creative.
- Some are compelled by images.
- Some are compelled by data.
- Some are compelled by interesting words and stories.
- Some are compelled by brevity.
- Some don't care, but they only read emails at 2pm.

Now, there are two reasons you write and send multiple emails.

1. You'll never send an email that everybody opens, so sending multiple emails gives you multiple chances to get your content in front of more eyes.

2. You'll never send an email that everybody likes, so sending multiple emails gives you more chances to connect with prospects in their love language.

And those are the only reasons you need to write an email drip campaign like this.

Your boss might come back and say *"you can't send this email. It only 1 of our USPs, and you know we have at least 3 really good USPs for this product category."*

You can reply with a confident *"I've planned for that. USP2 is going to get an email next week, and another in 6 weeks, and another in 9 weeks. And not only will those emails reach our prospects, but some of them will respond to the email filled with data related to that USP. Some will respond to the visually attractive email outlining the USP. And others will love the USP-related story in the last email. We're covering all USPs as well as every customer's stylistic preference."*

So here's an example of your planning for the 7 emails:

Email 1:

A nicely designed, long-form email that teases all the different sections of the permission asset blog and encourages them to click through to read the blog.

> **Why?** You want the reader marked (pixeled) so they are later treated to the relevant remarketing you're running.

Email 2:

A plain text email that tells the reader you just finished creating a cool new piece of education they might be interested in, with a single in-text link directing them to the squeeze page.

Why? You want to increase trust with your audience, and this appeals to the cynics.

Email 3:

An attractive informational email with a few datapoints from your permission asset, linking to a product page related to the data in the email.

Why? You want to increase trust with your audience, and this appeals to the cynics.

Email 4:

A part of a story from your permission asset. Linking to the squeeze page.

Why? Capture the part of your audience that likes a good story. Draw in a prospect that might be closer to in-market than they realize. Convert them to an active lead.

Email 5:

A brief plain text email with a compelling piece of data from the permission asset (a graph if available) and a link to the appropriate product category.

Why? Appeals to your audience with limited time and attention. Appeals to the data-driven reader. And works toward the average of 7 touchpoints brands need to get a result from a prospect.

Email 6:

A newsletter-style email with content curated from the permission asset (similar to email 1). Links in each section go directly to the blog.

> **Why?** Because the newsletter style is trustworthy and certain readers are more likely to click, get pixeled, and receive remarketing. They'll also trust you a bit more because of your awesome content.

Email 7:

A minimalist email with a single image from the permission asset, an anecdote, and a call to action to learn more by downloading the permission asset.

> **Why?** It's another good touchpoint. It's memorable because it's minimal. It could spark that procrastination gene and encourage the reader to get something they've been putting off done (like purchasing your services).

What do you do with your 7 ideas now?

You put them into a literal calendar. Don't store them in your head or in an email.

We use Google Sheets, with a new tab added annually for that year's content.

You can use a paper calendar on your desk if you want. Just as long as you write it down.

Here's what it can look like:

MAY

Sunday	Monday	Tuesday	Wednesday	Thursday	Friday	Saturday
1	2	3 Education #2	4	5	6	7
8	9	10 Rotovaps #2 Pharma	11 Chemistry	12 QC+R&D All other	13	14
15	16	17	18	19	20	21
22	23	24 Water Puri#3 Chemistry List	25 Microbiologist Environmental	26 Lab Managers All others	27	28
29	30	31 Spray Dryer#3 Manager				

JUNE

Sunday	Monday	Tuesday	Wednesday	Thursday	Friday	Saturday
			1	2	3	4
5	6	7 Edua #3 Pharma	8	9	10	11
12	13	14 Rotovaps #3 Pharma	15 Chemistry	16 QC+R&D All other	17	18
19	20	21	22	23	24	25
26	27	28 Spray Dryer#4 Lab Manager	29 Pharma All other	30 Food Health		

Something to remember:

Once you've built it you can do this over and over and over again. Nobody is going to remember that in September of 2024 they got the same email as they did in December of 2023. It's not a sneaky or dishonest move. You put a lot of energy into making these assets (the emails, the permission asset itself) and you deserve to have them out there.

How to learn more about the people you want to communicate with in these emails.

So remember, we're giving people different types of content based on what we think might motivate them to take action.

And you might think *I just work at a medium-sized business. We don't have the budget to do serious market research and sit people down in Mad Men style focus groups to find out if they like Young Sheldon and live in a condo!*

But you shouldn't think that. Because you live in the future and so many things are possible.

You don't get just one shot. You're sending a steady flow of emails. You get lots of shots. In the case of these permission asset emails, you have 7.

And you can make those shots count by qualifying your assumptions about your audience with tools you already have access to right now. You probably have a tab open with at least one of them on your laptop downstairs.

Get all the qualifiable information you need by looking into LinkedIn and Facebook's ad targeting platforms now. *Right now!*

As of summer 2024, here's how you find really useful info about your prospect demographics in LinkedIn.

Note: Below we show you how to get audience info from your preexisting email contact list. Your audience list could also come from your website visitors if you were ahead of the game and installed the LinkedIn tracking pixel previously.

To get info about your email audience:

- Export your email list to a spreadsheet, then sign in to your LinkedIn Campaign Manager.

- You'll see *Plan* in the menu on the left side of the screen. Click that.

- Then click *Audiences.*

- Next, you can click the Create dropdown in the top left corner.

- Below *Upload a list,* select *Company / Contact.*

- Give your audience a name like *Contacts from Email Database 2024, choose your List type,* and click *Select list.*

- Click Upload.

Now you can see information about your audience under the Audience tab.

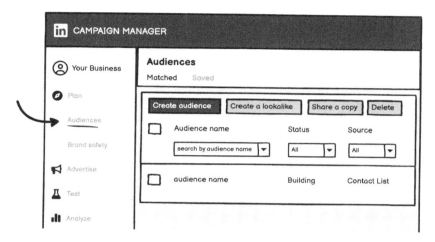

Now, whether you already had the pixel on your website or you just uploaded your email contact list, you can get a good idea about your audience.

Click on *Insights.*

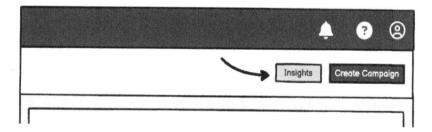

You'll see things like agriculture and farming, robotics, social issues, all aligned with a percentage that indicates your audience's affinity toward that specific interest.

If something's 50% or above, that's a high affinity and definitely worth working into your email.

So let's say you sell agricultural products, and you see your audience has an affinity for robotics. Maybe the visual assets in your email could take on some sort of technical and natural contrast. Like a robot butterfly gliding over a canola field. Or they like sports and entertainment. So you can built your content around generational sports accomplishments.

Don't take these insights lightly. These are the things most of your audience really care about. Work only makes up a portion of their lives. And while your primary interest is their life at work, you can connect with them over common interests (even if that common interest is gleaned from analytics).

Here's how you find really useful info about your prospect demographics with Google.

Like you did with LinkedIn, export your email list. Then upload the list as an audience match in Google Ads.

Click to "data insights" and select the segment you want insights on from your customer match list.

From here you can get all the basic firmographic information on your subscribers. Their gender. Age ranges. Are they a parent?

Probably the most interesting data is below in two tabbed sections, one called **in-market segments.** And one called **affinity segments.**

The in-market segments data means the groups listed below are areas in which the audience members are actively looking to purchase, so *they are in the market to purchase the things listed below.*

Here's a screenshot of an audience of prospects from a scientific equipment manufacturing company under the in-market tab.

Relevant segments

People in your data segment are most often associated with the following segments

In-market segments   Affinity segments

Select segments to add to an ad group

In-markets audience segment	Index	Size	Added to
Travel > Trips by Destination > Trips to the Middle East & Africa Trips to South Africa	5.9x	60M-65M	None
Computers & Peripherals > Computer Accessories & Components Memory & Storage	4.7x	100M-150M	None
Business Services > Business Technology > Enterprise Software Collaboration & Conferencing Tools	4.4x	150M-200M	None
Software > Design Software Drawing & Animation Software	4x	150M-200M	None

There are words and there are numbers. The words indicate things they're actively shopping for - like trips to africa and drawing and animation software. The numbers indicate the increased likelihood someone in that group has to be shopping for that product over an average person across the list. So in the screenshot, there's a 5.9x propensity to be actively shopping for trips to South Africa compared to the average person.

Here's a screenshot of the same audience under the affinity tab.

In-market segments   Affinity segments

Select segments to add to an ad group

Affinity audience segment	Index	Size	Added to
Shoppers Value Shoppers	2.1x	300M-350M	None
Shoppers Luxury Shoppers	2x	550M-600M	None
Lifestyles & Hobbies Green Living Enthusiasts	1.8x	450M-500M	None

You can see other information about them *in general.* This is non-commerce activity. It's the type of content they consume as they navigate the internet.

You can see they're value shoppers and green living enthusiasts.

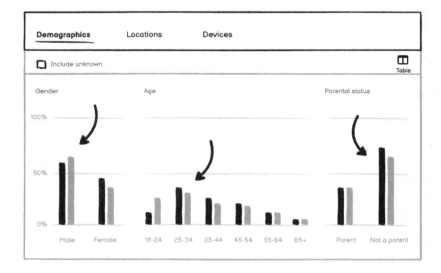

You can also see the average age range is mature at about 25 to 44, which corresponds with what we can see in LinkedIn as well (based on their job seniority). Turns out it's not just college students who care about value and green living. Even folks in established careers in product manufacturing like a good deal.

So if we cut back to our primary purpose here (the emails), it might make sense to lead one of your emails with a header image including a person sitting on a classic camping chair at the side of a river with a steaming coffee in the morning sun, their hiking boots to the side and the edge of a bright green tent peeking into the side of the photo.

The people who open that email are likely to see or feel themselves in that image, and if you can find a way to connect that image with clever text to what you're actually doing in the email, it'll have a huge impact on the success of that email via engagement and your perceived brand value with that audience.

Here's how to find really useful info about your prospect demographic with Facebook

You know how this goes if you read the last two sections.

Export your contact list, then add your list as a Custom Audience in Meta Ads Manager.

You enter your account, click to Audiences, then:

1. ***Create audience.***

2. ***Custom audience.***

3. ***Customer list.***

Select the identifiers to include, add the contact list you exported, and give it a name like *"I'm learning how to do this 2024 and hope I don't break anything"*.

Confirm that you mapped your identifiers correctly or resolve whatever errors show up (you'll get a green checkmark if your identifiers mapped correctly and you'll see a yellow exclamation mark if something seems off to the system).

Now you just click *Upload* and create.

Facebook will take a few minutes to hash your audience (hashing is a security thing to keep contact data safe) and give you a notification when it's done.

Here's what it looks like when you're done:

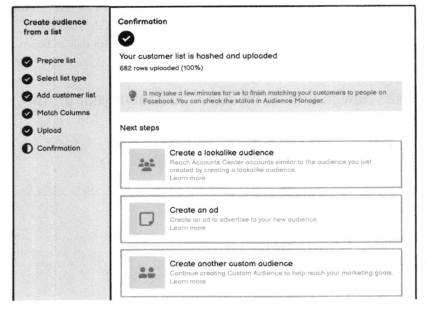

This all takes a little time to do. But once it's done, you can reference it easily and eventually it'll be stored in your brain so you can put other content together quickly or provide valuable insights to other members of the business.

Doing these things increases your powers significantly.

- You know more about the business.
- You're more valuable to the business.
- You can increase your results (and your salary) quickly.

It feels good to be powerful!

So you can use those insights to differentiate your emails with qualitative and quantitative information. But that's not the end of it! You're going to make the best calls to action - or is it call to actions? - CTAs you've ever seen.

Earlier (on page 116) we talked about the ways different people are engaged.

But they're still not going to do anything unless you tell them in a compelling way.

There's only a small percentage of the world's population that wants to:

- Download a PDF.

- Sign up to get something in their inbox.

- Click through and fill out a form.

- Set up a Zoom meeting with you.

- Reply and start a conversation.

And if you want the truth (which you do!) those calls to action aren't going to get people to jump.

So there are two things you can do to make them more enticing while still getting the outcome you want.

First - make the language on your call to action buttons better.

Second - support your CTAs with detailed info that puts the reader at ease.

Let's start with the first one. What kind of language makes call to action buttons better?

Some readers don't want to commit so hard. Downloading a PDF or signing up is a hard commitment. It's big! It's official.

Instead, *Learn more in this free guide.* Or See *how you can save time & stress here. Or Make your decision fast and easy with this guide.*

Or maybe your email doesn't solicit a download or a sign up (not every email in the permission asset sequence needs to seek a download).

Maybe you want to book a meeting over Zoom to talk over the problem the reader has that's related to the permission asset.

To some of us, booking a meeting doesn't seem intimidating at all. To others, it is impossibly intimidating. The kind of thing that nobody would willingly walk into. The scariest scenario.

But a chat is good. It's informal. There's no pressure.

So if your CTA is Find time for a quick chat on my real-time calendar here, instead of Book a Zoom meeting now, you're likely to have better results.

Think about the minimum viable commitment and make that your call to action.

It's fairly self-explanatory, but the minimum viable commitment is the smallest commitment you can ask for that will still achieve your goal.

It's small, unintimidating, enticing. You aren't asking for a lot of time, or mental energy, or anything else from the prospect. Just the amount you need to show them the value you have.

It's like the old 5-minute rule. If you're putting off doing something because of the time it conceivably could take to complete, just do it for 5 minutes. Often, starting is the thing holding you back, and you'll commit more than the 5 minutes you fooled yourself with.

With the minimum viable commitment, you're helping your prospects get past that tiny hurdle so they can benefit from what's on the other side.

Some marketers will fight tooth and nail saying you need to be extremely assertive with the words on call to action buttons in an email. For some audiences that does work. And there's no reason you can't try those types of CTAs. They're easy and straightforward. And even if you weren't Claire the Creator, you could still conjure them up in a second. But generally people rebel against the kind of authority those CTAs exude. Generally. So lean toward the minimum viable commitment.

Now for the second one. How to support your CTAs with detailed info that puts the reader as ease.

What does the reader need to feel comfortable in taking the action you ask them to take?

Here's an example.

- You want the reader to book an appointment with you over Zoom and talk about their problem (which is related to your permission asset because the content in the email was built around it), so you can show them how you solved it for other businesses.

Here's a problem:

- Nobody wants to take any action that is going to lead to an unqualified, unskilled sales person nagging them to learn more about products.

To avoid that reaction from your prospects, you can be very detailed about what the next steps look like to reinforce your CTA.

Call these reassurance statements when someone in your organization asks about it and make it abundantly clear that you know what the heck you're doing!

In the example above, those statements might look like this:

- When you schedule your chat in our calendar, we'll make our most senior expert in XYZ available.

- Jim Jimmerson has worked with businesses in XYZ industry for almost 20 years now, so he'll join you for a one-on-one chat.

Visualize what the next steps are. What it looks like after they take the action you want them to take. And use your words to make it comfortable and appealing.

It's going to increase the percentage who not only complete this action, but follow through and show up with their best intentions.

Remember, your prospects don't want to download something in general. They want to read something. Or they want to appease their appetite for reading by simply downloading it, with plans to *read it later* (only about half of downloaded PDFs actually get read).

Maybe they are open to downloading it once they're past that initial step of clicking the button in the email because now they've gone too far in their mind and there's no turning back.

The same goes for the landing page. If your audience has been sent to a landing page from the email and you want them to download something on that page, encourage them to read or learn or explore or get a benefit of some sort from the content - not to simply download. Downloading is a use of energy, mental resources. They will need to remember that they've downloaded something to later remove from their computer. Your prospects might not actively think these things. But the sentiments live in their unconscious.

You just want them to read and learn and act.

And that's everything you need to think about and do when you repurpose this permission asset content into emails.

You know your goals for these emails. And you know how many emails you're going to send out, on what days. You have the content ready (or at least some good ideas about the content for each email).

Wait! There's one more thing.

Once a prospect takes the action you want them to take, should they stop receiving these emails?

Like so many things, there are two schools of thought.

Yes and no.

Yes.	No.
Remove them because you aren't going to sell them the same thing twice, and they already moved past the email-action step in the buying cycle.	If someone makes a big deal about receiving an email about something they already did, do you really want that person as a customer?
If they keep receiving the emails, you're going to put them off and lose the sale.	After the last action they took, maybe they got distracted. They got busy. They fell off the horse and need help getting back on again.

You get to decide.

There are dozens of ways to remove users from an email campaign. And there are dozens of email services out there, so we can't give specific help with this.

But if you can't figure out an automatic way to remove the prospect after they take an action, you can always remove them manually at the end of every work day.

Curators can create emails from existing content.

You don't have time to dive into audiences and demographic info from multiple sources.

But you still need to create a sequence of emails to send to your audience over the next 3 months.

And they still need to appeal to different types of people in your audience (go back to page 116 to see the quick bullet points outlining the different ways you can do this).

So <u>your first step is creating a simple email sending calendar in a Google sheet</u>. You can go back to this page 119 for an example.

And your emails can follow the same content format as the Creator's emails. You can find those just below the example above.

You don't, however, need to create any additional original content for these emails.

Your permission asset is full of all kinds of informational tidbits your audience will enjoy.

And anywhere Claire the Creator is asked to make a fancy design, you just use the existing templated designs in your email marketing tool.

So you picked your top 7 tidbits and built them into the calendar, then follow these steps.

1. Open your email marketing tool.

   a. The business probably already has an account with Constant Contact, Mailchimp, Hubspot, Omnisend, SendGrid, or MailerLite.

2. Choose one of the template styles you like.

3. Using images from your permission asset and one of the informational tidbits you picked moments ago, complete the email template exactly as it is (replacing the placeholder content in the email with your own content).

4. Schedule your email to send based on the calendar you created in your Google sheet (all the email services mentioned above have a "send now" and a "send later" option once you've created your email, so you can set your date and forget about it).

When you're writing within the existing email templates in your email marketing tool, the most important thing is to remember what action you want the recipient to take from the email (and we've told you exactly what you want with each email in the Creator's section you revisited earlier on the last page).

In less than 1 full working day, you have 3 months of audience communication planned, scheduled, and off your mind.

Charles the Conductor - evaluate your Creator's email marketing approach competently.

You don't always know how exactly the email strategy for something like a permission asset should be done to achieve the results you want for the business.

It's been a long time since you got your hands dirty in Mailchimp, if you ever used an email marketing tool at all.

And you don't need to take on the responsibilities of learning how it will work, technically. Because you have other responsibilities.

But you now have the tools to evaluate your team's strategy, approach, deployment, whatever you want to call it.

If you gave them this book, you can go back to page 115, take 10 minutes to read Claire the Creator's section, and compare it to the output they're giving you.

If they did the work on their own, here are 4 questions to ask yourself as you review their work.

1. Is it clear what they're asking the reader to do in this email?
2. Would you click/take the action?
3. Is it clear the Creator thought about the audience when composing this email?
4. Is the email free of errors? (you'd be surprised, or not maybe, by the errors that can sneak into "final" drafts).

The goal of your drip email sequence (that's what this is, a series of emails that drip out to your email audience over a period of a few months) is to give the audience value, keep you in their minds, convince them you're the business to work with.

If you can't see those goals in the emails you're provided, send them back to your Creator with instructions from **www.jbbgi.com/resources** - you can copy and paste and edit in your own Google doc or right in your email to Claire the Creator.

The best thing you can do is competently evaluate your Creator's work, and the simple tips you just read are all you need.

Chapter 12

PUT EVERY NEW PROSPECT AT EASE FOR THE NEXT 6 MONTHS WITH 30 MINUTES OF WORK.

You can easily make 20 good quality social media posts from a 1,500 to 3,000 word permission asset.

Do you really need to talk about this on social media?

Yes! Because most B2Bs don't promote their permission assets well on social media. Or they do it once. One measly social media post about this awesome piece of content.

It's like putting your best sales rep on one phone call before leaving them alone in the back of the office filing papers.

Claire, here's the easiest workflow to get these posts live.

1. Open up the Google doc where the text of the permission asset lives.

2. Open a second Google doc and give it a title like "Permission asset X social media posts"

3. Highlight and copy the exact words from your permission asset that will form the main body of the social media post.

4. Paste those words into your second Google doc.

    a. **If you have access to a graphic designer,** using the comments function, add a comment that describes the type of image you would like - detailed instructions make it easier for your supporting digital team to bring your idea to life.

5. Do this as many times as you want.

6. Open up the Google sheet you used for your email calendar (back on page 119 we talked about this).

7. Slot in the social media posts over the next 8-12 months, making sure every time an email goes out, a new social post also goes up.

8. Stick to the plan!

Suddenly, you're doing omni-channel marketing. You're further reinforcing your message where your customers are.

Want to be sure those same customers who open your email also see your post on LinkedIn when they sign on later in the day? Go to page 120 and learn how to do it.

Chris the Curator, here's what you can do to keep the social media posts flowing.

You can keep a steady flow of social media posts pointing to your permission asset in about 5 minutes of work monthly.

1. On the first day of every month, open the permission asset.

2. Find a passage of text you like in the permission asset (ideally you pick text that's broken up into short sentences, so when you post it can look like this:

Your Company Name
100 followers
3mo Edited

What good is a larger ultrapure water filter cartridge?

Well, if it's filled with the same filter media (which it has to be, since it's ultrapure), it reduces your cost of ownership.

Want to learn more ways to reduce that cost of ownership?

3. Paste that text directly into your social media post, and put quotation marks at the start and the end.

4. After the last line copied from the permission asset, add *Want to learn more?* Or *Sound like you?* Or *Interested?* And paste a link directly to your landing page or the blog where the full text of the permission asset is posted.

The thing about social media for B2B is that it doesn't have to be done perfectly.

Often, **all you need is good enough.**

Charles, here's what you should do.

As is usually the case, you can do this two ways.

1. **Make social media posts a deliverable for your Creator from the start.**

    You can give them the instructions from page 136 of this book and when they submit the posts as part of the final deliverable package, it will be easy for you to spot check whether they followed the directions or not.

2. **Post these regularly yourself.** If you use social media regularly. Personally. You can take control of your social media presence and do the posts yourself. Most Conductors won't want to do this, but there's no reason you can't. It's fast, you know the parts of the permission asset that stand out to you, and your prospects, and you already have access to post behalf of the business*.

Don't already have access? You might get even more reach from your post if you make it on your personal LinkedIn profile, and simply tag your companies page so it appears in the main feed. LinkedIn tends to favor posts by people vs brands by rewarding them with further organic reach, meaning, more people see your post in their personal feeds.

Like we said, you don't have to be doing explosively innovative things on social media as a B2B. Just posting useful information from your permission asset will put you ahead of the majority of your competitors, if not all of them.

And something else: a lot of the time, **new prospects will visit your social media pages to calm their concerns about your legitimacy. If they see you posting regularly, they're more likely to become a revenue-generating customer.**

So easy posts generated from your permission asset have an often intangible but substantial value to your business.

Generating social posts from your permission asset with AI

Claire, Chris, and *Charles* can all use AI to easily generate loads of social media posts from blocks of permission asset content.

Here's how:

- Write this prompt into ChatGPT - "You are the social media manager at a B2B manufacturer. You recently wrote a piece of educational content for your customers. You would like to promote this on LinkedIn. You will now generate 10 social media posts for LinkedIn from that content. Each post must have a call to action, hashtags related to the content, and a link to www.yourlandingpage.com. Here is the content: *paste a block of interesting content from your permission asset here.*"

- Repeat this with additional sections of text from the permission asset.

- Paste the posts into a Google doc, and insert them into your social media schedule (in your Google sheet with your email marketing schedule)

Chapter 13

USE YOUTUBE TO MAKE YOUR JOB EASIER.

You saw this at the start of chapter 9 and we bet it gave you some anxiety.

After all, making and publishing videos is one of the hardest things to do. Right? …Right?

The fact is, **this isn't super hard.** It's all in your head (and your competitors' heads, because they sure aren't making videos beyond boring product presentations).

It's actually no harder to repurpose your permission asset content into a YouTube video than it is to repurpose it as a blog. And you already know how easy that is. Maybe you even did it already! It's another great way to move your prospects down the sales funnel.

If you feel you have more of a face for radio, never fear. You do not have to put your face on video to make a YouTube video - even a video that requires a talking head. But we'll get to that in a minute.

First, the options if you are willing to put your face on camera.

- Wistia
- Canva
- Pictory

But now that we've given you those options, we're going to steer you toward Pictory.

It's the easiest by far. You can make really good videos from your permission asset in ¼ the time of any other software available.

If we were writing this book 4 years ago, this would be a long section about the different tools and different approaches Creators, Conductors, and Curators should use to turn permission asset content into video content.

But since Pictory launched in 2020, we feel strongly that it's just about the only tool anybody needs to make this kind of video.

And we're sorry if this reads like an advertisement. It's just that Pictory does the job really, really well and the cost is low. Small businesses can easily find space in the budget for it (especially given that 1 additional sale to a lead that comes from your video will pay for your annual Pictory subscription 5+ times over).

How Creators, Conductors, and Curators can turn permission asset content into really good <u>talking head style</u> YouTube videos in less than 2 hours.

We're going to assume you took our advice and subscribed to Pictory for its tiny monthly cost.

You also have a subscription to Canva, because it's easy and you use it over and over throughout this book.

So, you're going to use Canva's Record yourself feature (because it optimizes the file size of the video very well) to record yourself reading the permission asset to your webcam.

Get yourself to a nice bright spot in the office, lots of natural light.

Put your permission asset on the screen, directly under your webcam.

Navigate to the Record yourself feature in Canva.

Step 1

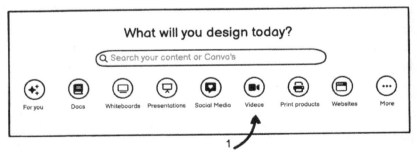

Step 2

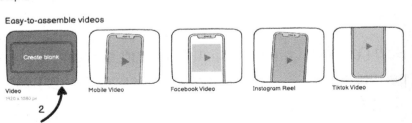

Step 3 and 4

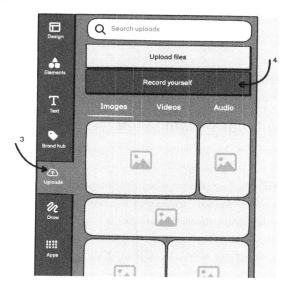

And hit record to capture yourself reading through the permission asset.

All you have to do now is:

- Upload your recorded video to Pictory.
- To do that, you look for the purple *Edit video using text* box on your Pictory home page.
- Click *Proceed*.

The software will read and understand your video, generating a script that runs alongside it. You can use the interface to remove pieces of video you don't like simply by removing the text from the AI generated script.

That's honestly all it takes. You can export the video and upload to your YouTube channel. You can paste the first page of content from the permission asset into the video description. And you have a talking head style video of your permission asset content.

(As a bonus, you can use Pictory to break your large video into small snippets, which you can post on your social media channels for something that really stands out among B2B social media posts).

How Creators, Conductors, and Curators can turn permission asset content into really good videos YouTube videos <u>without showing their faces</u> in less than 2 hours.

Maybe your face is actually the face of your side hustle brand, where you make sour cupcakes or lifelike object-shaped candles on the weekend. Maybe you just don't want to be the face. And you don't have to.

For this section, we're going to give 3 options. But we think these are all equally awesome. And it's up to you to decide what you want to use.

- Pictory.

- Synthesia.

- Doodly.

What's the difference?

Pictory lets you create videos quickly straight from the blog you posted of your permission asset, or by pasting the content of your permission asset into its *Script to video* tool.

It has a giant library of B2B images, and it applies those to your video based on AI interpretation of the content in your video. It makes remarkably accurate interpretations of most content, and you get a video with a voiceover and a string of interesting, related images in minutes.

Synthesia is far and away the best way to get a talking head video without anyone in your workplace serving as the talking head.

And without taking 20-30 minutes to record a video.

Synthesia converts your permission asset content into a script that's read by a real-looking AI avatar.

You'll think we're making this up when you see the quality of the avatar. It must be some sort of motion capture done by real actors. But it's not. It's just that good.

Here are two pro tips for Synthesia.

1. You can set your avatar inside a facility like your customers might work in, or recognize, with the built-in greenscreen feature. Find a video of the setting you want (using your Envato Elements account) and insert it behind your avatar. Your video is instantly more relatable.

2. If your avatar is struggling with the pronunciation of unusual words, words unique to your niche, write them phonetically in the script. For example, instead of jbbgi.com, you would write jay-bee-bee-gee-eye-dot-com.

Doodly creates doodles. Videos of drawings that go along with your text.

You can record yourself reading your permission asset directly in the Doodly app, and build a video in a few hours (Doodly says 15 minutes, but your permission asset is probably 2,800 words, and that takes a bit more time to bring to life).

And just like the previous section on the talking head style video, all you really have to do is paste your permission asset content into the software.

There are some prompts to follow when making your video with each platform.

But they're prompts. They're straightforward, and you don't need us to tell you here when you'll see the exact same things as you login to your Pictory, Synthesia, or Doodly account.

Posting your video to YouTube and doing more with it after it's made.

Posting the video you made to YouTube. Oh what have you gotten yourself into! Another of these things most people think is far more complicated than it actually is.

See the little video camera icon on the top right of the screen when you're in your business' YouTube account?

1. Click that.

2. Click *Select files.*

3. Choose your video file.

4. Add a title (like the title of your permission asset)

5. Add a description (like the intro of your permission asset, or the first full page).

6. Follow the prompts (it'll ask you if the video is appropriate for kids, and a few other things).

7. Complete the upload.

That's all you have to do. It takes less than 3 minutes.

This huge, seemingly insurmountable process of creating a video and uploading it to YouTube is completed, start to finish, in less than a day. If you're speedy, it's done before lunch.

And here's a really neat bonus.

You can then take your video and embed it on product and category pages using the embed code built right into YouTube.

Step 1

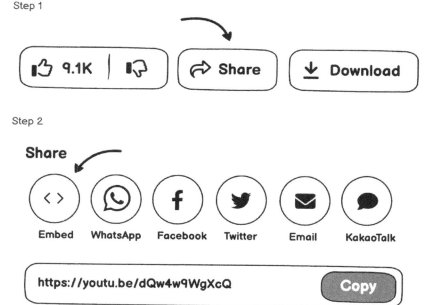

Step 2

So you're increasing the quality of the pages on your website by adding relevant video. You're giving prospects another element they might relate to/connect with. And you're doing cool work that your competitors aren't.

You're chasing away your imposter syndrome, or you're helping your staff rise above theirs. You're doing great work.

Chapter 14

STOP FREAKING OUT ABOUT SOCIAL MEDIA.

You're going to encounter plenty of charlatans who say the most important thing is to grow your social media following to tens of thousands of "people" or accounts.

We throw those quotation marks around "people" because there's no way Jim's Asphalt and Shingles has 20,000 followers on LinkedIn or Facebook.

19,906 of those "people" are not real.

There is no value in a bloated, inflated social media following.

Over the last decade we've onboarded dozens of B2B customers who want to "continue to grow our social media following." Almost without fail, these customers have worked with an agency in the past that bought social media followers to inflate their own invoices.

Yes, you can spend a few hundred dollars and get a few thousand new followers on your preferred social media platform. But your return on investment is going to be precisely $0.

So why bother with social media at all if you aren't chasing a large following?

Proof.

Proof to your prospects that you're still relevant. Still in business. Still engaged with your customers, however few actually follow you on social media.

We (or more accurately, you) provide that proof by repurposing your other content (like the permission asset content you spun into social posts in chapter 12).

Lots of B2B companies hire younger staff with previous experience in B2C. And they think social media is the answer.

They push hard for more energy to be directed into social media (even if they aren't in the marketing department).

For most B2Bs, this means paying salaries for people to engage in a channel that creates very few real business outcomes.

The trickiest part of this for Charles the Conductor (and to a lesser extent, Claire the Creator, who shares workspace with these social pushers and Chris the Curator who works closely with them) is that it's easy for these new staff to dazzle with lots of vanity metrics. Things they can show and talk loudly about.

Like the 10,000 new followers they helped you land over the last 6 months, or the 150 likes or comments on their most recent post.

In almost every case, those aren't real metrics that are going to drive business

So how can you tell what's actually a great target to chase on social media?

Just look at the biggest brand in your space and their following on any social media platform.

Look at Thermo Fisher Scientific, for example.

For most B2Bs, Thermo is probably bigger than your largest competitor. It's a publicly traded company with over $40 billion in revenue last year and 130,000 employees globally. If you go to its Facebook page, you'll see tens of likes on every post.

Looking back to January 2024, the most engagement any post ever received is 41 thumbs ups.

Is Thermo putting out a weak social media effort? No. Because the reality is **it doesn't matter.** It doesn't matter if the company has 10,000 likes on each of these posts. Those vanity metrics aren't going to generate any additional business and revenue at the end of their year.
Every month, Thermo puts out <u>at minimum</u> a weekly post. Most of the time it's a post twice a week.

And that's what you should be doing too.

It tells your customers you're paying attention. You're alive. There's a channel where your customers can easily reach out to you, if they want.

But **you don't need to hire a full-time social media manager.** For most B2Bs, it's not a fulltime job. It's just repurposing existing content you've already written and pushing that out into social media.

It's the dozens of posts you can pull out of your permission asset (you learned about this in chapter 12).

But there's something else your team can do to make your social posts appear infront of more *actual* prospects.

Individuals in the business (even beyond the Conductors, Curators, and Creators like you) can casually use social media to act as force multipliers on any marketing efforts related to the permission asset (or anything else the business creates).

Here's how.

Go to Facebook and use the search box in the top left hand side. Search for whatever keyword represents your target customer. In the left column you'll see filters - including groups.

Take a look at those groups. There, your potential customers are joining together and talking about what they do with the products or services you sell.

So what do you do with this information?

A brand, as in your business' Facebook account, can't share the content you posted on your social page into these groups. It has to be done by an individual. A user account. This is why it just doesn't happen that often. And this is why it's a good opportunity for you. **Your competitors are not doing it.**

As an example, we searched for *wastewater treatment professionals.* Lots of B2B companies could sell into this group. The second group listed in the search results has 18,000 members.

Wouldn't you love for these <u>18,000 members</u> of wastewater treatment professionals to see the post about electrochemistry equipment that your business page shared and only 2 people engaged with last month?

Join the group with your personal account. Have other members of your team do the same. Usually there's a little form you have to fill out that asks why you want to join the group and confirm that you'll abide by the rules.

Then…

1. Go to your company's Facebook page.
2. Find a post on your page that is not sales focused (like one of the informational posts that links back to your permission asset blog).
3. Click the share button at the bottom right of the post.
4. Click the *share to a group* option.
5. Find the group you want to share to.
6. Add some additional text to give the post context - and include emojis and hashtags (don't worry, hashtags are easy to find. Just use the search bar in Facebook, type a word related to your permission asset, click posts, and scroll through the posts to see the hashtags other users are sharing).

Now your message is casually in front of many more people than ever before inside of your target market.

You distributed your omnichannel message organically. Nice!

If other members of your team are in the same groups, or actually joined when you asked, make sure they like and comment using their personal profiles within the first 24 hours of the share into the group. This will ensure as many of the group members as possible see that post.

We said it before. You aren't going to make a viral social media post. And even if you did, it probably wouldn't have an impact your business. You're niche. You're B2B. It's just not the right way to spend a large portion of your limited energy.

But you can increase the trust you have with prospects. You can find prospects with their guard down. And you can give them value, so they choose you when they're in market.

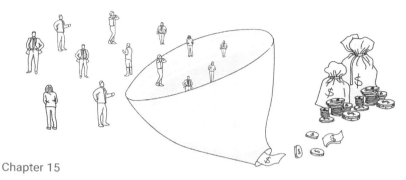

Chapter 15

STEP # 5. 10X THE EFFECT OF EVERYTHING YOU DID IN THE LAST 12 CHAPTERS.

Entice more and more visitors to download your permission asset every year for the next decade

Over the next 45 pages or so, we're going to show you exactly how to capture your leads by getting that permission asset downloaded, using assets deployed across your website.

You can call this…

On-site merchandising for your permission asset.

So let's start at the beginning.

On-site merchandising is used when there's something special to talk about. A promotion. A new product. A valuable piece of content like your permission asset.

The goal of your permission asset's on-site merchandising is to direct more people from one section of the site to the permission asset landing page.

It's about increasing awareness of something that could matter to the prospects on your website. About helping meet their needs, opening them up to your brand, and giving away value so they are more receptive to your products or services.

What kinds of things are valuable as on-site merchandising for a permission asset?

1. A home page banner.
2. A category page banner.
3. An inline banner.
4. A slide-in banner.
5. An exit-intent popup.
6. A chat automessage.
7. A blog post (and if you already did this, great!).
8. A landing page (and if you already did this, also great!).

If you're Claire the Creator, you can do all these things and you're about to see how. If you're Charles the Conductor or Chris the Curator, skip to page 172 (unless you're interested in reading about all 8. Then stick around).

Merchandising with a homepage banner

A homepage banner is a large "hero" image with a call to action at the very top of your homepage.

Ideally it's an attractive graphic with a compelling message and a call to action that speaks specifically to the pain or problem your permission asset addresses.

Some brands choose to place an image of the permission asset book on the homepage, followed by "download now". This idea is bunk. B2B is full of this and it's invisible to prospects.

We will almost always choose creative imagery to get permission assets noticed. With the advent of AI image generation, everyone has the ability to generate unique and compelling imagery, even if the subject of the permission asset is very niche.

For example, one of the images below is aided by AI, one is not. Can you guess which is which?

A quickie on AI image generation as of April 2024.

AI image generators are getting better fast. Crazy fast.

Right now, the best quality images come from a generator called Midjourney.

It's a bit complex to use. But if you're reading this and interested, learn more about how to get started at **www.jbbgi.com/midjourney**.

You can also experiment with Bing Image Generator, Dall-E 2 (which comes from OpenAI - the ChatGPT people), Crayon - all for free.

The thing to know is that better prompts create better images. Learning the language of prompts is a valuable future skill and we recommend spending time with it.

The messaging in your homepage banner should be benefits oriented.

Main heading = A big benefit statement. Like "Save Your Samples Before Disaster Strikes"

Subheading = Supporting info. Like "The real value of a new ultra-low temperature freezer isn't the energy savings. It's the protection your samples get from future failures."

Button = Action or pain. Like "I want to avoid lost samples" or "Learn how to shop for your next ultra-low".

Merchandising with a category banner

A category banner is similar to the homepage banner, but it lives on a category-level page on your website.

A category-level page comes after the navigation on your homepage. It's the bridge between your homepage and your product pages where viewer intent changes. If a visitor goes through to a category page, they're in-market. So the messaging should be different than your homepage banner

For example - you're a business selling mugs. Coffee mugs and beer mugs. But you have many models of coffee mug, and many models of beer mug. So from your homepage you can click through to either "coffee mugs" or "beer mugs". And from there, on those coffee or beer mug category pages, you run down your models.

The category pages help users intuitively navigate to products within those categories.

Alright. Now…

Your category banner sits at the top of a category-level page, and should use the same imagery as the homepage banner.

It should use different messaging than the homepage banner.

Why?

You want it to <u>look the same</u> because:

- Consistency is valuable. It moves you closer to those 7 touchpoints that can get your audience to act.
- A lot of thought goes into the visual representation of your permission asset, and this is one of the ways you get more return from your investment.
- You already decided on the best way to visualize the permission asset. If you need to come up with a different design for each merchandising point on the website, you're just diminishing the quality with each one.

You want to <u>use different messaging</u> because:

- The messaging you used in the hero image on the homepage didn't get the prospect to act.
- The mindset of a person on a category page is different than the person on the homepage. They're more clearly interested in this area of your products or services, so you can speak to them differently.
- It's easier to experiment with different words than with different imagery.

The homepage banner casts a very wide net. The category banner is a bit more focused.

For example:

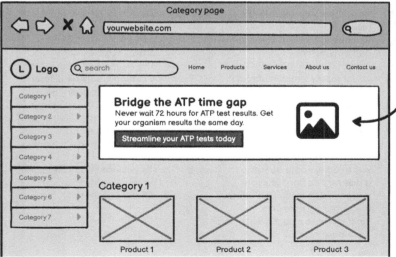

Merchandising with an inline banner

An inline banner doesn't sit at the top of the page like a category or homepage banner.

The inline banner is inline with the body of the page, so it lives somewhere further down on the page.

What page? It could be...

- A category page.
- A product page.
- A blog page.

Where does it go on that page?

10% of the time
Above the fold

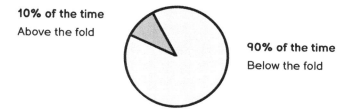

90% of the time
Below the fold

*Above the fold refers to any content that loads in the immediate viewing area when you click through to a new webpage. It's the most valuable real estate on that page, sort of. Below the fold refers to anything that requires scrolling to reach. You could argue that below the fold content is actually more valuable because readers who scroll are more engaged and more likely to convert. But that's an argument for another time.

And what exactly is it?

It's a banner, which you're familiar with.

It can follow the same appearance scheme as the other banners in the merchandising flow.

But it contains more information, because it's further down the funnel.

So you might give a more detailed explanation of what the user can expect by clicking on and engaging with it. You can tell more of a story because of this position further down the funnel.

This is why 90% of the time it goes below the fold. Because the user is revealing their location in the funnel by scrolling to look for more information. You give them what they want.

You can use words that respond to the context of the prospect's visit.

Because they know the very direct connection between what they're currently doing and the value this gives them.

Marketers often say clear beats clever every day. But there must be no immutable rules. In an inline banner you can be clever, playful. You can use jargon. You can make a bad industry-insider pun.

Here is an example of an inline banner:

Heading: Not Sure If A Plasma Cleaner Can Help Your Lab Run Better?

Subheading: Get Complementary Data to Help You Decide

Text: Our engineers put their heads together to bring you a comprehensive guide outlining applications that benefit from plasma cleaning, and how exactly you can qualify those benefits in your budget request. Get access to tips for planning ahead, the features that actually make a difference in your application, and the questions you should ask whether you choose to work with us or not.

Button: Read your free copy here.

Merchandising with a slide-in banner

A slide-in banner is a small box, maybe occupying 1/10 of the screen, that slides into the bottom left or right corner of the screen when a prospect lands on a given page.

Keep that consistent visual vibe with the rest of your merchandising assets.

And whittle the message down to the most direct form you can think of. You only have a little space to fit a few compelling words. So use it wisely.

The slide-in banner can also be used comfortably site-wide because it's unobtrusive.

A user can close it if it's not for them and generally that doesn't put them off whatever part of the buying cycle they were in.

It's like the Kit Kat bar at the checkout of the grocery store. A prospect might be on their way to completing a process or a purchase and this draws them into something else they know they need but weren't looking for in that moment. But now they're going to investigate. And they'll either increase their overall purchase now or return because the memory of that delicious Kit Kat (or your delicious permission asset) is fresh.

You can configure the aggressiveness of your slide-in banner in your SAAS tool (which one do we recommend? Go to **www.jbbgi.com/tools**).

The main one being: **How long before the slide-in triggers when the page is loaded?**

This is a setting measured in seconds that you get to control.

But what is the optimal amount of time to delay before the pop-up appears?

It's different for everyone, and here's how you figure it out based on data from your own customers in under 2 minutes.

1. Navigate to Google analytics.

2. Find the average customer's time on site.

3. Divide that by two.

That gives you the number of seconds delay the slide-in should wait before appearing to the customer. If someone is just navigating through a page, going from the home page to a category page and to a product page quickly, they're very unlikely to see the slide-in on the page where they had no intent on sticking.

This avoids wasting the slide-in on the knee-jerk reaction of someone just frantically looking to close any pop-up because they are not interested in the current page's content.

Adjusting this time delay setting has a huge impact on the success of the campaign, and it shouldn't be overlooked.

Merchandising with an exit-intent pop-up.

An exit intent pop-up appears when triggered by an action.

B2Bs aren't using these very often. Because they don't do everything they can to generate leads. But you've probably seen lots of consumer websites with these. You move your cursor to the top corner of the screen to close the web page and up pops a few words and a form.

Hey get 10% off if you give us your email

Don't forget to download this guide so you can make a more informed purchase the next time you come back.

The browser recognizes you're going to close the website and it's a last ditch effort to get a bit of information. To get the hooks in and encourage somebody to come back.

The messaging on an exit intent pop-up can be pretty aggressive because the prospect is leaving anyway.

What do you have to lose?

I f****** hate pop-ups

- The business manager reviewing the website before it launches.

There used to be nothing that could overcome this objection.

But since we live in the future, the technology you're using to display banners that slide in or pop up or hover over the screen all have an advanced rule set built into them. You can configure them (no coding, just click settings) to show a single pop-up, one time, to a specific user. After the user sees the pop-up one time and closes it, they'll never be bothered again.

As long as that cookie sits on their browser saying they *f****** hate pop-ups don't show them again.*

Over the last 5 years, we've rarely heard the surly manager complain about pop-ups. The ability to cookie users and hide popups based on that first interaction has breathed new life into this ancient online lead generating tactic.

Maybe dancing babies will come back one day too.

Reduce friction. Generate leads from your permission asset merchandising without pushing the permission asset download.

Your slide-in or pop-up doesn't always have to guide the user to your landing page.

The merchandising can be a conversion point itself.

If you're crafty, or have access to a web developer with the most basic of abilities, you can embed a form using custom HTML or a form builder. You can collect the user's contact information right there on the pop-up or slide-in with your campaign imagery above the form.

It looks like this:

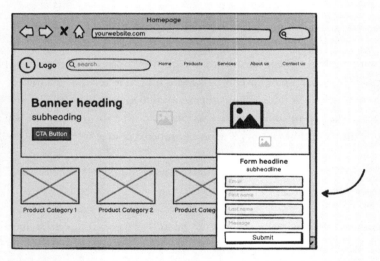

You can also integrate the lead collection data from your pop-up or slide-in SAAS with any modern CRM. So the information collected in the form is immediately put into a sales workflow or a targeted drip email automation or a text message followup automation.

When you reduce the number of steps needed for a user to declare their interest and intentions to you, you improve their user experience.

Reduce friction - increase sales.

Merchandising with a chat automessage.

Live chat is another fantastic tool that can get you permission asset-driven leads.

If you do it right.

The next time you look at your competitors' websites, make a note of their live chat.

- Is it dormant? (meaning it's just a little icon bubble in the bottom right hand corner of the site)

- Does it greet you? (and make you feel even the slightest bit drawn to writing something in there?)

- What else do you notice about it?

For most B2Bs, on-site chat scores lots of customer service related inquiries from existing customers. It's a reactive tool. A prospect is only going to use it if they're looking for a super easy way to contact the company.

It's not going to persuade anyone to start a conversation with the business unless it's proactive. And when you start looking at these on-site chats through the lens of reactive vs proactive, you notice very few companies use these tools to their best.

Most companies check a box by putting live chat on their websites. They don't optimize!

Oh boy. Are you ever going to optimize yours!

Every chat application from Olark to Intercom to Drift (even free ones like Tawk To) have a feature to enable proactive messaging.

What this means is when a user lands on a specific page, the chat automatically opens with a greeting you can customize.

Think of what's going on at your tradeshow booths.

What's the number one rule sales staff or customer support staff should follow when they attend a trade show?

Budget has been poured into this tradeshow. Exhibitor space, hosting prospects and partners, travel, accommodation. The promotion that goes into driving traffic to the booth.

It's a lot.

And the number one rule is *greet people when they walk by.*

Which is a problem, because it's not enough. And it's a bad rule. A simple hello gets you a head nod, or a hello back. It doesn't engage anybody.

If tradeshow staff open with an engaging question, like *Hi there. What type of tests do you run in your lab?* They're more likely to receive a more thoughtful answer. The person walking by has to stop, because there's more to think about than just *Hey.*

If tradeshow staff sit on their thumbs, waiting for someone else to open up the dialogue, the big tradeshow investment gives a poor ROI.

By having a reactive chat on your website, you're making the exact same mistake as above.

But I'm not at a tradeshow. What interesting proactive message do I have for prospects on the website?

What you have is a permission asset you poured a ton of resources into. And you want to give it to as many people as you can.

Proactive message:

- Hi. Hope you're having a great day. If you want help with your purchase but don't want to chat right now, this free XYZ buying guide will make your job easy. Just follow this link. And if you want to chat at any point, I'm Kora and I'll be here.

- Hi. Not sure how XYZ can help in your application? Here's a free case study that shows how other businesses have done it.

When a prospect lands on any product or service page related to your permission asset, they're greeted with a friendly pop-up offering free value.

Compare that to the messages you see in the chat on most of your competitors' sites, which only pop up after you click the chat icon (unlike yours, which is configured to pop up proactively):

- Hi. Our customer support agent is online to help you today.

- Hi. Let us know if you need a hand.

With the proactive message approach, you generate leads from your permission asset in two ways.

1. You get downloads that can be followed up on.

2. You get more chats than most B2Bs.

And the chats generated by this approach are unlike any chats captured before.

Now it's a lead generation tool. A sales tool. Not just a customer service tool.

There was a time when we used reactive messaging in the chat applications on client websites. It was a long time ago. We've grown up since then. But there was a time. And **what kinds of improvements did switching from reactive to proactive make?**

The dramatic kinds.

B2B websites with a large volume of traffic (say 20k per month) that traditionally only got two to three inbound chats per day saw the number of inbound chats increase by an average factor of 9. Some increased by 20X and 30X.

Live chat vs chatbots

If you're not using live chat on your website because the business doesn't have the humans to manage it, you should ride the AI wave.

Live chat is great. But it consumes resources. And AI is quickly replacing the need for a live agent in most situations.

Tools like Journey AI (**www.jbbgi.com/journeyai**) can help your customers find products or services they need in plain language - even if they don't have a clue what they need.

Your business can program boilerplate content into the end of Journey AI's intelligent responses. These boilerplate blocks of text are originally intended for legal disclosures in sensitive industries, but can be repurposed for lead generation.

For your customers, Journey AI just recommended the right product. Then it closed with a boilerplate message "to validate this selection, check out this guide. You'll learn exactly why this was chosen for you."

Of course we recommend Journey AI over any alternative. We built it exactly for you because there wasn't a suitable option available.

<u>But at this point in your merchandising, a problem exists.</u>

It can be overwhelming and off putting when competing interactive elements on your website keep popping-up and getting all up in your customers' faces at the same time.

We don't have a rule for you to follow about the number of pop-up elements you can or cannot have running at a time. This is all for your judgment.

Test. Go through your website like a first time user. Like a **real first time user.**

Do you use Chrome or Safari on the regular? Then open up Firefox or Internet Explorer. Open up an incognito tab. Start going through your website like you've never been there before.

Each time you exit from a pop-up, close that window and open a new incognito window to continue your tests so you see the full extent of your merchandising campaigns.

You might notice the chat pop-up on your site conflicts with your merchandising pop-ups, for example, and you'll need to adjust one or the other to avoid coming across like a 1996 Atlantic City casino.

Don't forget to do this on your phone too!

Follow the same steps as above. Clear your browsing data.

But I don't want to do that. The cookies on my phone make life convenient!

You got that right.

So download a secondary browser to your phone and have at it.

The user experience on your phone could be very different from your laptop or desktop. Pop-ups and slide-ins don't always work well on mobile devices. Luckily, you continue living in the future and this is a super easy fix. Every tool you could be using for this (including the one we recommend at **www.jbbgi.com/tools**) has a setting to avoid showing pop-ups on mobile.

It's actually a standard practice in our workflow to disable these pop-ups on mobile devices. But if yours looks slick, it's up to you.

Merchandising with a blog post.

Hold on. You already made your permission asset into a blog post, right? Using one of the methods we talked about back on page 108?

But here's a little detail you may have missed. And it will help you engage with your internal resources, like web developers, whether you're Claire, Chris, or Charles.

Maybe one of your imposter syndrome challenges is dealing with website resources. You're no expert. But you have to know some basics so you can communicate with the people who do have the expertise.

Ask the person who maintains your website this:

- Is there a configuration option we can enable with a couple clicks to get blog entries on related product or product category pages?

    o   *make sure this is a no-coding option. Just clicking settings. Custom coding breaks things. Your developers will always say yes, they can custom code it. But don't pursue that option. Please don't pursue that option.*

Most current website builders have these configuration options.

If for some wacky reason you want to do this yourself (**Claire, we're looking at you**), the main, general steps to follow are:

1. Write your blog.
2. Tag your blog (if it's about veterinary ultrasonic cleaners, tag it something like "veterinary ultrasonic cleaners." Creativity.).

3. Post your blog.
4. Make sure the blog module on your category or product pages is configured to display based on tags.
5. And make sure your product or category pages are also configured to display blogs based on the tag you just created.

Why do I need this blog to show up on these pages?

Because you're adding variety to your lead generation strategy. You're creating more opportunities for revenue growth.

On your homepage you might have a "latest news" section with the most recent blogs published for everyone to see. But eventually your permission asset blog will get pushed out of that section of the website. It'll disappear to most people.

By putting it on related product and category pages, you're keeping a valuable piece of content visible to the audience that cares about it most.

Maybe they weren't interested in downloading it based on your inline banner. But they're into blogs. They're more likely to click through to read more if it's in blog format. Maybe their affinity for blogs makes them more likely to download the full text of the permission asset from the links embedded in the blog you posted.

And now you have their information.

Here's another thing. The leads you get in the first quarter after you launch your permission asset amount to about 10-15% of the total leads your permission asset will generate over its lifetime - if you merchandise it with these evergreen tactics. The magic is in the implementation, not just the creation.

Merchandising with a landing page.

You already built the best landing page ever based on the rundown back on page 88.

Most of your other merchandising sends prospects to this marvel you created.

There's nothing else to do but sit back and watch the leads flood your inbox.

How can Conductors spearhead the right kind of merchandising?

You've probably heard this before. It might be something you struggle with. But as a Conductor, you're most powerful when you work on the business, not in the business.

That means **building a standard operating procedure (SOP) for merchandising your permission asset** so your Creator (and others in the business) can follow and take the burden off your shoulders.

You don't want to find out 12 months after your first permission asset goes live that it's generated precisely 0 leads because nobody knows about it. Because all your team did was make it and drop it on a landing page before sending a single email about it. But this is honestly where most employees stop, wipe their brow, cheer about a mission accomplished, and move on to the next thing.

What a waste of something that could generate leads for a decade if implemented correctly!

So with an SOP in place for merchandising, you can make sure everything gets done properly and your valuable permission asset is working day and night to generate your leads.

You don't have to do anything other than read and understand the one we've built for you. Then tell your team it's how things will get done from now on.

You can to **www.jbbgi.com/resources** to download and **print a checklist to give the Creator on your team**, plus download and **print the instructions from Claire the Creator's section of the merchandising chapter** so there's no confusion about what they need to do.

As a quick reference, at this point Claire the Creator needs to make:

1.   Home page banner.

2.   Category page banner.

3.   Inline banner.

4.   Slide-in banner.

5.   Exit-intent popup.

6.   Chat message.

They also should have made a blog post (refer back to page 108 about the blog post) and landing page (refer back to page 88 for about the landing page) earlier in this process.

You already gave sufficient direction earlier in the process to align the permission asset's positioning with your personal experience. And that direction should carry through the merchandising for the permission asset as well. **No need for you to give further direction on this to your Creator.**

Now, *any time you launch a new permission asset, there's no discussion about what needs to be done* to make sure it generates loads of leads. And there's *no confusion* over expectations surrounding a permission asset project.

Plus, one of the best parts of making this SOP the go-to for your permission asset merchandising is:

Measuring and managing the output of your Creator employees becomes easy.

You don't have to trust what they say about the completeness of the task. The checklist is either done or it's not. And the assets either line up with your early instructions about positioning or they don't. It cuts your time and energy investment by 90%.

Tips to make sure this is done right.

When you're verifying whether your new SOP was followed, we recommend:

1. Using an incognito web browser to view the website (and the merchandised content) like a prospect.

2. Using your phone to view the website (and the merchandised content) like a prospect.

Tests to make sure this is done right.

When you're verifying whether your new SOP was followed, you should test 3 things:

1. Complete the form on the landing page. Does the lead actually show up in the appointed inbox? (either a general sales inbox or the inbox of a staff member responsible for managing leads).

2. Download the PDF. Is it the correct permission asset? Does the download actually work?

3. Engage with the chat automessage (or AI, or live chat). Does appropriate messaging show up on appropriate pages? And do you get the expected response from your bot, AI, or staff?

4. Pretend you're going to close your incognito window. Does the exit intent popup appear on the appropriate pages?

When it's implemented correctly, you'll see leads start rolling in. But more importantly, the leads will continue, and even grow, over the next decade. Tracking alongside your growing revenue.

And how can <u>Chris the Curator</u> merchandise permission assets?

Curators like you might not have the time to implement the creation of a full suite of merchandising assets.

If you have to implement everything in sporadic blocks of time outside your main duties, you have to prioritize what will give the most value with the lowest time and energy commitment.

We recommend prioritizing like this.

1. Making sure your permission asset blog automatically updates in the blog template on your product and category level pages.

2. Activating the homepage banner.

3. Activating the category banner.

4. Updating your chat automessage.

5. Activating the slide-in.

6. Activating the exit-intent popup.

7. Placing the inline banners in content across the website

Your main objective is to get the maximum amount of merchandising up on your website with the minimal amount of effort.

So, you need to:

- Design your merchandising assets.

- Deploy your merchandising assets.

- …as quickly and easily as possible.

There is a single tool you can use to activate your handle slide-in, inline banner, and exit-intent popup. It's called OptinMonster.

There is a separate tool to design your banners and other graphic assets. It's called Canva.

The tool to use for live chat, and to update your automessage in, is Olark. Unless you're upgrading to AI chat. Then your best choice is Journey AI - since we built it to fill a gap that existed in the B2B market.

So now that you know the tools. Let's address each of the 7 pieces, in order of priority and ease.

1. Making sure your permission asset blog automatically updates in the blog template on your product and category level pages.

This is easy and quick.

Ask the person who maintains your website this:

- **Is there a configuration option** we can enable with a couple clicks to get blog entries on related product or product category pages?

- *make sure this is a no-coding option. Just clicking settings. Custom coding breaks things. Your developers will always say yes, they can custom code it. But don't pursue that option. Please don't pursue that option.*

Most current website builders have these configuration options.

If for some reason you want to try this yourself (maybe to get more familiar with the inner workings of the technology supporting your workplace), the main, general steps to follow are:

- Write your blog (you already did).

- Tag your blog (if it's about veterinary ultrasonic cleaners, tag it something like "veterinary ultrasonic cleaners." Creativity.).

- Post your blog (you already did).

- Make sure the blog module on your category or product pages is configured to display based on tags.

- And make sure your product or category pages are also configured to display blogs based on the tag you just created.

2. Activating your homepage banner

You have to do three things to get the homepage banner on your website.

Create the image. Add the text. Put it on the website.

If you have access to a graphic designer on your team, they will create it and add text. You just have to tell them the type of image you want. For some details about that, you can flip back to page 154.

If you have to create it yourself, here are the steps.

Step 1. Choose any of the images you used in your permission asset.

Step 2. Prepare a blank document in Canva

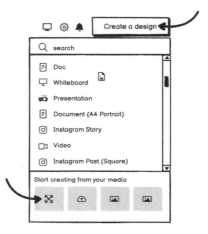

Step 3. Choose your banner image size. One of these:

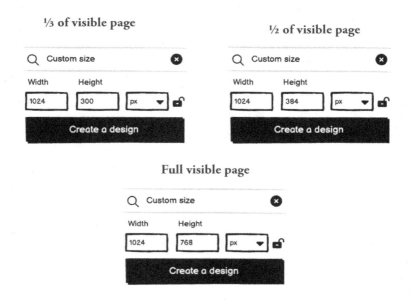

Step 4. Click *Create new design*

Step 5. Since you already used Canva to create your permission asset design, all your images are already available in the *Uploads* tab. So you can choose your image and drag it into your pre-sized homepage banner box. If you haven't, you can just click *Upload files* and choose an image from your computer.

Step 6. Click the *Text* tab and experiment with the font you want to use in writing your banner message. There's a section back on page 154 about the messaging for your banner.

Step 7. Download it (that's under the *Share* button on the top right of your screen) and upload it to your website.

Step 8. Place it on the homepage of your website. We can't say exactly how to do this, since there are so many services you might be using. But, in general, you can simply drag and drop it into the hero section of your website in the front end designer.

Step 9. Link the image to your landing page (note that you don't have to link JUST the button. In many cases, the button you created on your banner image is just part of the image, and clicking anywhere on the image will lead the prospect to the permission asset landing page. The button design, as it were, is just some psychology to use on your prospects).

And now you're done with that.

3. Activating the category banner

For the theory behind your category banner, you can go back to page 156.

If you just want to get it done (which you do), here's the Usain Bolt version.

Step 1. Duplicate your homepage banner image.

Step 2. Type new text into your existing text boxes, taking into consideration the more obvious intent of anyone who will see this banner (they've already clicked into the product category on your website, so they're in-market).

Step 3. Follow all the steps to download the image you just made and upload it to your website.

Step 4. Place it at the top of the category page to which it belongs.

Step 5. Make sure it links to the permission asset landing page.

Now you have merchandized category banners. Nice work!

4.   Updating your chat automessage

You might have already read about updating your chat automessage if you're thumbing through sections for your Creator colleagues.

There's a great rundown of how you can update your automessage on page 165.

Here's your checklist to make sure you do it right:

- Have you enabled proactive messaging (this is whatever setting your chat app has to open the chat automatically when a user lands on the page)?

- Have you updated messages on product and category pages related to your permission asset using the examples on the previous page?

Then your job here is done.

5. Activating the slide-in.

Your slide-in banner is powered by OptinMonster (OIM) or your website's native popup app.

If nobody on your team has set it up, you can go to the OptinMonster website to get started. Any guide we could give you here would be a copy of the already excellent user tutorials available from OIM.

To design your image for the slide-in, follow the steps you used to make the homepage banner, but change the dimensions to 350 x 350 pixels.

6. Activating the exit-intent popup.

Your exit-intent popup is also powered by OptinMonster or your website builder's native popup app.

So you can create it the same way you created your slide-in. Add your campaign imagery, some text, a form field, and a call to action.

Here's a wireframe to give you an idea about how it can be designed.

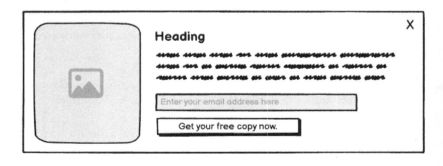

And here are the 4 steps to setup the rules so it displays at the right time, when a user is on their way to close the browser.

- Find the *Display Rules* view in the campaign builder.

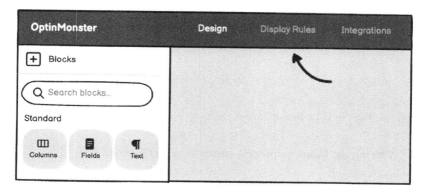

- Choose *When (Triggers)* from the menu on the left-hand side and pick the Exit-Intent option.

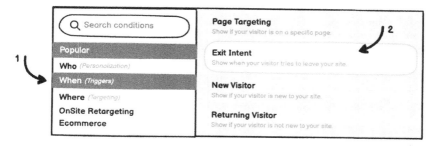

- You can then choose which devices your popup should display on and the sensitivity you would like to use (choose medium sensitivity, and display on desktop devices).

- You can also choose the pages where your slide-in appears. For your first permission asset, it should appear everywhere. But as you create more permission assets, you should make sure the slide-in is restricted to pages where users would expect it. If you sell lab baths and rotary evaporators, and your permission asset is about rotary evaporators, don't leave it to display on lab bath pages after you create your lab bath permission asset.

And your exit-intent popup is ready to go live when you hit save.

You just have to click to the *Publish* menu to publish it.

7. Placing the inline banners in content across the website.

You're familiar with OptinMonster or your website's popup manager at this point. So you know you can simply choose *Inline* when you create a new campaign, and that will create your inline permission asset merchandising banner.

But there's one important difference between your other OptinMonster banners and your inline banner.

All your other campaigns are set up using display rules. The display rules dictate where they will show up on your website.

Inline banners have to be placed manually, by copy+pasting code into your website back end.

The code is generated by OIM under the Publish menu when you get to that stage, under a big yellow block of warning text, so you can't miss it.

But if you aren't comfortable working with code in any way, it's better to stay away from this step, or get a helping hand from someone with a little experience.

If you are, then you just have to paste the code into the space on the page where you want the inline banner to appear.

And with that, you've completed all the merchandising your permission asset needs.

Every prospect coming to your website now has a much greater chance of converting to a lead.

Over the next year, it's not unreasonable to expect this merchandising to 10X the number of leads your business collects.

We have clients who built a half dozen permission assets 5 years ago and collect a volume of leads that increases every year passively. They don't do any big marketing pushes. They occasionally update the permission assets with valuable new information their customers might like.

Their sales team has a constant flow of leads to follow up with. Their marketing team has time to think deeply about product positioning and data to support the next big thing in the business.

This up-front merchandising work pays off for a long time. It's a convincing sales rep that gently encourages your prospects to lower their guard and bring you into their inner circle.

Chapter 16

OVERCOME YOUR GREATEST FEARS WITH PAID ADS.

We don't expect you, Chris and Charles, to roll up your sleeves and build out a campaign of paid ads to generate leads from your permission asset.

You should task your Claire the Creator or your favorite marketing agency (**www.jbbgi.com**) to do it.

Some Creators can, and we'd like to help more Creators find their footing with paid ads.

In this section, we're going to tell you how to create your paid ads on the most valuable ad networks for lead generation with your permission asset:

- Google.
- Facebook.
- Linkedin.

And we're going to tell you to the best of our ability what makes a good one, and what makes a bad one.

We say *to the best of our ability* because there are always anomalies. Outliers that defy common sense. And it's always good to experiment to see if you can uncover one such lead generating anomalie.

But it's also good to make sure you have a solid, reliably performing baseline. And that's what we want to help you get.

So let's start by setting up your Google ads account and building a basic campaign.

How to get Google Ads up and running.

Your customers are on Google dozens of times daily. Searching for things related to your business, related to their personal life, related to nothing at all.

They're there. It's why paid ads on Google are standard for lead generation (and lots of other objectives).

But, like the YouTube video from the previous chapter, it's intimidating. The interface seems large and technical. Daunting to use.

And it IS large and technical, because there's a lot that can be done with it.

Lucily, there's no reason for you to dive into everything it can do. For right now, you just need to do one thing - prepare a paid ads campaign on Google that drives traffic to your permission asset landing page.

And it's not only the leads that come in from your paid ads on Google. It's the fact that your prospects see your brand name when they perform relevant searches. It's an intangible benefit. We often see an ad through the day and go straight to the website without clicking the ad. It happens way more than you realize. So being visible on Google, providing free information to your customers, is about as valuable a thing as you can do.

Here's exactly how you set up your first permission asset lead generating campaign.

Step 1. Set up your account:

If you don't already have one, sign up for a Google Ads account at ads.google. com by clicking on Start now. You'll need to provide some basic information about your business and billing details.

Step 2. Set up your first campaign:

In your Google Ads account, click on the big blue + New campaign button to create a new campaign. It's in the left corner of your ads home page.

Then choose Sales as the campaign goal, then Leads as the campaign type. This will optimize for people signing up and downloading your permission asset.

Step 3. Choose your location targeting:
You don't need this explained.

Step 4. Choose your language targeting:
You don't need this explained either.

Step 5. Set your daily budget:

This needs a bit of explaining.

Your daily budget is the maximum amount you're willing to spend per day on your campaign. If you hit your budget, Google stops showing your ads, and the ads resume at midnight, when Google's day resets.

Budget doesn't carry over. So if you only consumed $10 of your daily $20 budget on Monday, you don't now have a budget of $30 on Tuesday.

In fact, if you see a string of days where you only consume half of your daily budget, you should just decrease your daily budget to match the trend you see.

You aren't charged the full daily budget if your campaign only spends $10. You're only charged for the clicks/impressions you get.

We recommend you start with a daily budget of $10 and see how you want to adjust after a few weeks there.

Step 6. Create your ad group:

An ad group organizes together similar ads under a common theme. You can name it something related to your permission asset.

But if I'm just making ads for my permission asset, why should I create an ad group?

Because one day you'll be running ads for more than just this permission asset. And being organized from the start will make your job easier down the road. It's like eating well when you're 40 so you don't have health problems at 60.

Every ad group you create can have different targeting, budgeting, independent reporting, and a few other useful items. Speaking of which...

Step 7. Set up targeting:

This is how you tell Google who you want seeing your ads.

There are 12 targeting options as of June 2024, including:

- **Keyword.** The most common form of targeting, where your ads show up based on searches related to your identified keywords.

- **Placement.** You can pick specific sites, pages, mobile apps.

- **Audience.** You can suss out users by demographics, interests, behaviors.

- **Geography.** Get your ads to show in specific countries, regions, cities.

- **Device.** Choose to display on desktop vs mobile vs tablet.

- **Ad schedule.** Control when your ads are shown by day and time (so you can capture more prospects during business hours).

- **Location.** Target ads to users in specific locations based on their physical location.

- **Remarketing.** Target previous visitors to your website.

- **Similar audiences.** You can find new audiences, similar to your existing audience.

- **Affinity audiences.** Go after users based on their affinity for interests and lifestyles.

- **In-market audiences.** Reach people actively searching for products/ services.

- **Custom affinity audiences.** You can create custom combinations of interests to target.

For your first go at this, start with keyword, geographic, and device targeting to reach your core audience. When you're more comfortable experimenting you can layer on additional targeting like interests, demographics, remarketing to further refine your campaign.

Google Ads has a built-in keyword research tool you can use to find relevant keywords to target for your campaigns.

To access it:

1. Log in to your Google Ads account.

2. Click the *Tools* icon.

3. Click *Keyword Planner.*

4. Enter your landing page URL and desired countries to get keyword ideas. You can also enter seed keywords (keywords you think users might be typing related to your permission asset product category) to generate more ideas.

5. If you want, you can use the filters and settings to narrow down keywords by monthly searches, competition, suggested bid, and more.

6. Save any keyword lists you make, because you can directly import them into your account for targeting.

Step 8. Set your bid strategy:

There are a few options, but the only one that matters to you is Maximize Conversions.

Google will automatically set bids to maximize the number of conversions for your campaign while spending your daily budget.

To select *Maximize Conversions:*

1. Edit your campaign or ad group settings.

2. Under *Bidding choose Maximize Conversions.*

3. Make sure conversion tracking is implemented on your site to measure conversions accurately (instructions in the box after this list).

4. Let the bid strategy run for a while and monitor performance.

How do I make sure conversion tracking is setup?

- In your Google Ads account, under the Tools tab, click on Conversions.

- Click +Add Conversion and choose the type of conversion **you want to track** (you want to track leads right now).

- Give the conversion a name, like PA - *Mercury Analzyers.*

- Click Add tag and copy the tracking code snippet.

- Go to your website and paste the code you just copied on the thank you page from your permission asset landing page form. Put it right before the </head> tag.

- Submit a conversion yourself to make sure it's being tracked accurately.

- Conversion data will start populating in your Google Ads account within 24-48 hours.

Step 9. Write your ads!:

Here are a few simple examples:

Headline:
Your Free Mercury Analyzer Buying Guide

Description:
This Free Guide Simplifies Mercury Analyzer Research So You Can Buy With Confidence. Get The Details Now.

Display URL:
www.yourcompany.com/mercury-analyzers

Headline:
Compare Mercury Analyzers Easily

Description:
Your Free Guide Has Everything You Need To Evaluate And Choose New Mercury Testing Equipment Fast. 2024 Edition Available Now.

Display URL:
www.yourcompany.com/analyzers-2024

Headline:
Mercury Analyzer Buying Simplified

Description:
Struggling To Research Mercury Analyzers? This Free Ebook Makes It Easy To Pick The Right Equipment Today.

Display URL:
www.yourcompany.com/mercury-analysis

Headline:
Stop Wasting Time - Get Your Mercury Analyzer Ebook

Description:
Cut Hours From Your Research Time With This Detailed Mercury Analyzer Guide. All The Data You Need In One Place.

Display URL:
www.yourcompany.com/mercury-ebook

These are simplified examples. But you can follow the fields included in your Google ads account.

The main things to remember are:

Simplicity rules. These are short ads, so there's no time to be fancy. Tell it like it is.

Title case rules. Start every word with a capital letter. It produces better results in every case study, so it works.

Step 10. Get approval:

Now you just submit your ad to Google for approval. This usually takes 1-2 days.

Fix any issues if the ad is disapproved.

Then feel proud that you just did something that's going to make you look really good to your manager, and you can tell your family about it after work.

How to get Facebook ads up and running

Facebook ads are never as successful at direct lead generation as LinkedIn ads.

But they perform another important role.

They keep you in your prospect's mind.

They remind your prospects about you even when they aren't thinking about work.

And, occasionally, they even capture new leads. But again, this is not their greatest power. The intangible effect of your presence in the feed of targeted prospects is what makes Facebook ads worth using.

So here's how you do it.

Step 1. Set up a Facebook Business Manager account:
Start by setting up a Facebook Business Manager account, if you don't already have one. Here, you'll manage all your Facebook advertising. Go to business.facebook.com and follow the prompts. It's as easy as anything you do online.

Step 2. Go to Ads Manager:
Once your Business Manager account is set up, go to Ads Manager. You can find it in the Business Manager dropdown menu at the top left of your Business Manager homepage.

Step 3. Create a new campaign:
In Ads Manager, click on the green + Create button. This will bring you to a page where you can choose the objective for your campaign. Facebook has a handful of default objectives - Awareness, Consideration, and Conversion. Your goal is to direct users to the landing page where they can download your killer permission asset, so you're going to choose Conversion as your objective.

Step 4. Choose your Ad Set:

After picking your campaign objective (Conversion, remember), the next step is to set up an Ad Set. Here, you lay out your target audience, placement, budget, and schedule.

- **Audience:** You can target based on location, age, gender, language, interests, behaviors, and connections. You can also create a Custom Audience (based on your email list or website visitors, which we gave you instructions for back in chapter 9) or a Lookalike Audience (based on similarity to your existing customers or leads).

- **Placement:** Decide where you want your ad to be shown. This can include Facebook, Instagram, Audience Network, and Messenger. We suggest you stick with Facebook. Generally, your demographic isn't heavily invested in Instagram, and the other placements just don't get traction in our experience.

- **Budget & Schedule:** Decide how much you're willing to spend on your ad campaign and when you want your ads to appear. Want a spend recommendation? Start with $10 per day and see what happens.

Step 5. Choose your ad format:

Next, you'll create your actual ad. You can choose from several different ad formats, including single image, video, carousel (multiple images or videos in a single ad), slideshow, and collection. You're going to use a single image ad.

The best Facebook ad format to use for B2B permission asset lead generation is by far the single image.

Here's why:

- Single image ads are the most common type of Facebook ad. People expect to see them, and indeed Facebook has spent a ton of time and energy optimizing the way they appear in the user's daily scroll. They're simple, but that's what works for them. They look great on both mobile and desktop. You already have several images that portray the value of your permission asset, so you don't have to do any challenging work to generate a new image. You just use what you already have. The text for your ad can come straight from your landing page, since you already communicated the best value proposition for the permission asset there.

Step 6. Create your ad:

Now you'll add the content for your ad. The requirements for this will depend on the ad format you've chosen. If you follow our recommendation with the single image ad, you'll have to upload your image and your text. Canva has a template for Facebook ads. When you click Create a design in Canva, a search bar pops up. You can type in Facebook and your first option will be Facebook ad, which is 1200 x 628 pixels.

Step 7. Conversion tracking with Facebook Pixel:

Facebook Pixel is a piece of code you place on your website to track conversions, optimize ads, build targeted audiences, and remarket to people who have taken some kind of action on your website. To create a Pixel so you can track these things, go to your Business Manager, click on Events Manager, then click on the green + Connect Data Sources button and follow the prompts.

It's just like the tracking you set up for your Google ads.

Step 8. Review and be done with it!:

Review all your ad settings and make sure everything is correct. If it all looks good, submit your ad. Facebook will review your ad and it will start running on the date you decided.

Keep an eye on your conversion data. You won't get as many conversions with Facebook as you will with your LinkedIn ads (next up). But you will still get some. And remember that the intangible prospect awareness is what really matters here.

How to get LinkedIn ads up and running

In many cases, paid ads for a permission asset on LinkedIn generate more leads than all other channels combined.

Specifically, it's the sponsored posts.

With all things being equal, and sponsored posts setup on all major social networks, LinkedIn sponsored posts directing traffic back to your blog or permission asset landing page can bring in 50-60% of your total paid advertising leads.

So if you're deciding which ad network to prioritize for this type of lead generation, prioritize this one.

Here's how you get yours up and running:

Step 1. Set up a LinkedIn Campaign Manager account:
If you don't already have a LinkedIn Campaign Manager account, you'll need to set one up. This is where you'll manage all your LinkedIn advertising. You can set up a new account by going to www.linkedin.com/ad/start. Follow the prompts to set up your account.

Step 2. Pick your LinkedIn ad objective:

Once you set up your Campaign Manager account, the next step is to create a new ad campaign. Start by clicking on the Create Campaign button.

This will bring you to a page where you can pick the objective for your campaign. There are a bunch of options, including:

- Awareness (Brand Awareness).

- Consideration (Website Visits, Engagement, Video Views).

- Conversion (Lead Generation, Website Conversions, Job Applicants).

In the context of this book, you're going after Lead Generation.

Step 3. Choose your target audience:

After picking your campaign objective, you're going to define your target audience. LinkedIn allows targeting based on characteristics like location, company size, industry, job title, job function, skills, education, interests and so on. Be as specific as possible to ensure your ad is shown to people who are most likely to be interested in the permission asset.

Step 4. Pick your ad format:

You can choose from a handful of ad formats, like Sponsored Content, Message Ads, Dynamic Ads, Text Ads, and Video Ads. Each format has its own advantages and is suited to different types of campaigns.

- Sponsored Content: These ads appear directly in the LinkedIn feeds of the professionals you're trying to reach. This is what you should do.

- Message Ads: You can send direct messages to your prospects with personalization. Hey Ben... type messages. These can also work to generate leads with your permission asset.

- Dynamic Ads: Don't bother.

- Text Ads: These are simple, and we like simple. But we've seen limited success using these to generate leads with a permission asset.

- Video Ads: Most small to medium sized B2Bs think they don't have the resources to create these. <u>But that doesn't mean you can't do it.</u> You could find a video in Envato Elements if you opted to sign up earlier in the book. You could place some simple text over the video using Canva, and you could post that as your video ad, linking to your permission asset landing page. Or you could use one of the short social media clips from your permission asset video if you already prepared those (as simple as a click using Pictory). **Think of how cool that would be.**

Step 5. Set your ad placement:

You can choose whether you want your ad to appear only on LinkedIn (this is the default option), or also on LinkedIn Audience Network, which are partner apps and websites where LinkedIn ads can appear. With your first permission asset, there's no reason you can't test the audience network. But we have seen limited results from it.

Step 6. Set your budget and schedule:

You probably already decided how much you want to spend on your campaign. Now you can choose to set a daily budget, or a total budget for the life of the campaign. You also need to choose your bid type (cost per click - it only costs budget when a user clicks - cost per impression - a lower cost, but it's incurred every time your ad appears on a screen - or automated bidding - which mixes the two in an attempt to get you the best value) and set your bid. The higher your bid, the more likely prospects are to see your ad over competitors'.

Like your other paid ads, start with something like $10 per day and see what happens.

Here is where you also set a schedule for your campaign. You can start your campaign immediately or schedule it to start next week, or next year. You can also set an end date or let it run until you manually stop it.

Step 7. Create your ad:

Now it's time to actually create the ad. This process will vary slightly depending on the ad format you picked earlier. In general, you need to create compelling ad copy and include a strong call to action - which you already did several times before now with your permission asset. You're an old hand at this. Use some of your preexisting messaging and pat yourself on the back for doing such an awesome job a week ago. **Your sponsored content will look just like the social media posts you created earlier in this permission asset merchandising process. So use the post you think is your best.**

Step 8. Review and launch your campaign:

Give your campaign a once-over. Make sure everything you set up makes sense. If everything looks good, click on the *Launch Campaign* button to start your campaign. It will be reviewed by LinkedIn and, assuming it meets the company's ad policies, it will start running on the date you specified.

Step 9. The optional-but-not-*really*-optional step. Conversion tracking:

If you want to track conversions (like you are for your other paid campaigns), you'll need to set up conversion tracking. This involves adding a LinkedIn Insight Tag to your website. Here's how you do that.

The tag is a piece of JavaScript code you add to your website to enable conversion tracking and website retargeting.

Start at your LinkedIn Campaign Manager and click on the *Account Assets* dropdown. Then choose *Insight* Tag.

Follow the prompts to set up your tag. You'll be asked to name your tag and add your website domain.

Once you're done with the prompts, LinkedIn will generate some code for you. The *Insight* Tag code.

This code needs to be added to the thank you page for your permission asset download, ideally before the end of the </head> section.

Most website builders now have a section in the settings where you can easily add the code. If you aren't comfortable with this, find yourself someone who is.

To **verify your tag has been installed correctly**, you can use LinkedIn's Insight Tag Helper browser extension. You install the extension in your browser before visiting the page where your tag is set up. The extension will indicate whether it's working or not.

Once the Insight Tag is added to your site, you can set up conversions.

In the LinkedIn Campaign Manager, click on the *Account Assets* dropdown again, but this time pick *Conversions*.

Click on the *Create a conversion* button.

Name your conversion and define the conversion action (*PA - Mercury Analyzers* makes sense for you), and specify the conversion method - choose *Event-Specific Pixel*. The other option needs more work, and this works just as well.

Assign your conversion window. This determines the timeframe LinkedIn uses to track conversions after someone clicked or viewed your ad. You can choose a window anywhere from 1 to 30 days for post-click conversions and 1 to 7 days for post-view conversions.

Choose your attribution model. LinkedIn lets you select the attribution model that best suits your campaign. We like *linear*. It's simple and easy to interpret.

Click save! And give the thumbs up to your closest colleague.

And there you have it. You're now running LinkedIn paid ads. And yours are better organized than every one of your competitors. Way to go!

With the combined forces of all your new paid ads, you will be generating more leads weekly than you did last month.

And the beauty of these paid ads is they also take customers away from your competitors.

Most B2Bs don't do paid ads well. The people putting the ads together don't understand the audience, don't understand the business. Don't understand the pain your prospects have.

By following the steps from page 1 to this page, you built an infrastructure that innately supports better paid ads. And that investment will pay off in leads that quickly convert into customers for life.

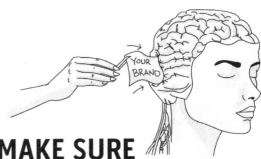

Chapter 17

STEP # 6. MAKE SURE CUSTOMERS AND PROSPECTS NEVER FORGET YOUR BRAND + BUY FROM YOU TWICE AS OFTEN.

You didn't think you'd just hoard these leads for a rainy day, did you?

Here's what you've done so far as you followed your stream through this book.

You made (or got made) a great permission asset that will generate leads for the next decade.

You posted (or got posted) that great permission asset as a blog, so it can bring traffic to your website for the next 10 years.

You made (or got made) a great landing page that will convert better than most in your industry.

You made (or got made) a ton of valuable merchandising that will drive traffic to your permission asset landing page for years.

You made (or got made) all the pieces you need to collect more leads this quarter than all of last year.

You have a large, evergreen campaign you can deploy again and again without any more work.

But…you aren't going to sit back and wait for those leads to convert to customers, are you?

Good, because if you did, we'd have written this chapter for nothing. Here are some interesting facts we turned up from Hubspot.

- 72% of companies with less than 50 new opportunities per month didn't achieve their revenue goals,

- 15% of companies with 51 to 100 new opportunities didn't achieve their revenue goals.

- Just 4% for companies with 101 to 200 new opportunities didn't achieve their revenue goals.

With more opportunities it becomes increasingly likely that you'll achieve your revenue goals. In fact, **it becomes almost impossible that you won't.** Achieving those goals makes your company more formidable, more stable, more valuable. Makes your job more secure. Makes your salary bigger.

But you have to proactively go after those opportunities.

Large companies have dedicated teams of Sales Development Representatives (SDR). Their only job is to book appointments for the sales team. To take leads, wherever they find them, and get those leads talking to seasoned sales professionals.

Most small to medium enterprises don't have a full-time SDR team. Most, like yours, send those leads straight to experienced sales reps. And that actually takes away from their ability to do their best work.

Your sales reps might spend around ⅓ of their day talking to actual leads. Where does the rest of the time go?

- A little over 20% goes to writing emails.

- 17% goes to entering data.

- Another 17% of the day goes to prospecting and researching leads.

- 12% goes to internal meetings.

- 12% goes to scheduling calls.

What you have to do is build a system to nurture the leads collected by your permission asset (and eventually, assets), so the lead is red hot by the time they first communicate with your sales team.

Then, your sales team is talking to hot leads for a larger portion of their day, not prospecting and researching and writing emails and entering data and scheduling calls that go nowhere.

You can automate this whole process and chase down these leads at scale, fire them up, by following the steps you find in this chapter.

You're going to get:

1. More proactive appointments booked for your sales team.

2. And you're going to maintain better contact with your existing customers, which leads to unearthed sales opportunities, unrelated to your permission asset.

What exactly am I going to do now?

You're going to write (Claire), generate (Chris), or assign and evaluate (Charles) short, plain text emails inviting your prospects to communicate and let down their guard. And your ultimate goal is booking sales appointments (although you'll never call them that).

These emails are going to:

✓   Appear personal and human.

✓   Be brief.

✓   Come from an email sender that's not your usual marketing sender.

✓   Be plain text.

✓   Contain dynamic text (like the lead's name).

✓   Multiply the revenue generated by your permission asset.

What is my goal with these plain text emails?

To get a response from as many contacts in your database (new leads and existing customers) as possible.

And for leads to book sales appointments on a real-time calendar so your sales team can do more of what they love (and generate more revenue).

What else do I need to know before doing this?

You're going to send these emails from a phantom. A fictitious member of the staff at your business with a job title that screams helpfulness to your contacts.

So you'll choose a full first and last name, you'll create an email account that follows the same conventions as other emails in the business (for example **johnbuie@jbbgi.com** or **jbuie@jbbgi.com** or **john@jbbgi.com**). You'll authenticate this email address with your email marketing platform. And you'll use this email sender for all your plain text emails.

The last thing to know is that you can do this three ways.

#1. You can send this nurturing campaign to all your contacts - those who downloaded the permission asset and everyone else in your database. All your current customers. Cold customers. All of them.

The main benefit of this is the unexpected sales opportunities you'll unearth from existing customers or cold customers. And of course you nurture leads who downloaded the permission asset more closely than you otherwise could.

#2. You can send this nurturing campaign only to the leads coming out of your permission asset download.

This way, you can target them very specifically with questions about the permission asset and their application. This kind of targeting produces better results than option #1. But with a smaller audience.

#3. You can do both. A nurturing campaign for your permission asset downloaders with specific messaging related to the permission asset and their application. And a parallel nurturing campaign for your existing contacts, where you speak more generally about problems they might have.

We recommend #3. But you might choose one of the other options based on your resources. It's up to you.

Claire the Creator - here's how you build your nurturing email campaign.

We're going to start with 2 templates you can follow for your first email. One is for your existing customers and cold customers. One is for your permission asset downloaders.

You can complete them with details relevant to your business.

You'll notice a few things about them.

1. They're short. But it needs to be. Contacts don't always receive your emails while sitting at their desks. And on their phone, they aren't going to read a long block of text. Your message needs to come fast and clear.
2. They contain a real signature, just like a real person! Prospects are more likely to respond if they think it's a real person on the other end.
3. There's no teaser text to go with the subject line, unlike the marketing emails you send. Why? Because humans don't write teaser text in their emails. They just write the email.

Here are your 2 templates.

Subject:
Need a hand with (SOMETHING RELATED TO YOUR PERMISSION ASSET) FIRST NAME?

Hi FIRST NAME.

It's not every day you're tasked with investing in a new ITEM FROM PERMISSION ASSET CATEGORY.

If you spent all your time thinking about them, like I do, it wouldn't be such a pain.

But since you don't, I'd love to help you get this done quick so it's off your mind.

What exactly are you using your ITEM for?

Ben Benson
PRODUCT CATEGORY Application Expert
COMPANY NAME
EMAIL ADDRESS
PHONE NUMBER

Subject:
Carrying stress home from work, FIRST NAME?

Hi FIRST NAME.

Hope you had a great weekend.

I wanted to drop you a note today because I just got off the phone with a customer who waited 3 business days last week for a response from her regular SUPPLIER OF X. She still hasn't heard back.

And when she finally does, she knows it'll be an email. Not a real, helpful person on the phone.

So she called us. Got on the phone with SALES PERSON NAME right away. And had A SOLUTION/WHAT SHE NEEDS within 2 hours.

2 hours!

She's not carrying that stress home with her at the end of the day again.

And now she knows she can call SALES PERSON NAME again any time and get a quick resolution. No stress.

Do you have a ticket you're waiting for another provider to solve?

-Ben (OR WHOEVER YOUR PRETEND SDR IS)

Ben Benson
Customer Assistance Escalator
COMPANY NAME
EMAIL ADDRESS
PHONE NUMBER

When you pretend SDR gets a response from a contact, it's the job of the person or people monitoring that inbox (more on this on the next page) to nurture the contact down the funnel.

Remember - the goal after getting that initial response is to move the prospect toward a sales call.

So let's say you get that response from a prospect about their application. You can respond to them saying something like Oh interesting. I'm not as familiar with that as my colleague Rick so *I don't want to lead you astray. Can I have Rick give you a call at 1pm today?*

You could also direct the prospect to choose a space on Rick's real-time calendar if that works for them (every CRM today has this feature). But promising a call at a specific time makes it deadly easy for your prospect, so we often recommend that option.

The response must be another exercise in restraint. Just like the initial email. If products in the category are on sale, don't mention that in the response. Don't push for the sale in any way. Just offer help. Free value. Nothing more. It goes against the instincts of every sales professional in your business, but it's important to stick to the approach. The gentle nurturing is why it works.

Using the templates provided, you can build out a total of 12 emails to your existing contacts, and 12 emails that go to every lead generated from your permission asset.

You can build them as marketing automations in your email marketing platform and set a rule that the prospect is removed from the automation when they complete the preferred action (responding to the email).

Now, when you write these emails, they will change slightly with every iteration. And the final email in the series will look very different from the first. But remember:

- Stick to a single message.

- Lean on the USPs you developed in chapter 3 of this book to develop your messaging.

- Think about the problems your customer might have and offer help.

- Resist the temptation to build a monument to your product or service benefits in these emails. **We repeat: stick to that single message.**

Your schedule for sending this nurturing campaign.

Choose a schedule that doesn't conflict with the permission asset email send schedule you created in chapter 9.

Leave 1-2 weeks between email sends, so you aren't driving your contacts away with excessive neediness.

However, there's something else worth thinking about. And we don't have the exact answer for you. But your sales team can't handle a huge influx of appointments at once. They lose the ability to respond to customers quickly.

So you'll have to spread out your email sends. Break your list up by some sort of characteristic you already have tagged in your email marketing platform. If your contacts are tagged by some subcategory, try that. Or by location.

With that done, you can now maintain a steady stream of nurturing contacts at scale. You free up your colleagues in sales to focus on the actual sales, not the early stage nurturing and development.

You contribute to their success alongside your own, since their compensation is often directly tied to sales, and yours is not (although your case for a big salary increase grows as they make more sales based on your nurturing strategy).

And with this nurturing campaign running, you're doing more than every competitor on your horizon.

The Curator's path to building a nurturing campaign.

You read the introduction earlier in this chapter, so you know the idea behind this nurturing campaign.

Since this is not your primary job function, building these types of campaigns, we recommend you create one single nurturing campaign for all your contacts.

Later, when you have capacity - like in 12 months - you can use the method outlined in the coming pages to create a nurture campaign just for your permission asset leads.

But for the sake of your sanity, right now you can focus on just 1 campaign.

You're going to use ChatGPT or your preferred AI to generate these emails for you, and you're going to rely on the mind map you created in chapter 4 to prompt the AI effectively.

Back then, you mapped features to benefits. And those benefits inherently solve a frustration.

So you're going to ask your AI to write brief emails about those frustrations, ending each email with an open ended question to which they can respond.

Or you're going to use the template below to write your own, following the same pattern but with different frustrations taken from your mind map.

Here's an example:

> **Subject:**
> Hey FIRST NAME. What's your risk tolerance?
>
> Hi FIRST NAME.
>
> How much $ do you think human error costs your workplace?
>
> For one of our clients in X INDUSTRY, a single TYPE OF ERROR last year cost about $5 million.
>
> To make sure it never happens again (or at least to get the absolute best chance that it won't happen again), we helped them automate several repetitive steps in the APPLICATION.
>
> Machines don't get as casual as humans do after running through the same steps 50 times.
>
> There might be similar easy ways to reduce the risk of human error (or other risks) in your workplace.
>
> I dare you to stump us with your problem!
>
> Where are you seeing those costly recurring errors?

In that example, the frustration is human error and the financial cost incurred. But you could easily change it to human error and the time burden incurred. Or human error and the workplace culture hit. Or human error and the logistical challenges of product recalls.

From that single template with a single frustration you could turn out 4 valuable emails that touch on exposed nerves for your prospects.

You can follow the same pattern and niche down your frustration.

Maybe the frustration is sharing equipment in their workplace. Maybe the frustration is working long hours because there is too much demand on existing infrastructure in the business. Maybe the frustration is managing the budget with a supervisor breathing down your prospect's neck.

There are dozens of frustrations you can work with inside this template and it may be less effort to simply adjust the template yourself than using AI to write them for you.

So **if you choose to use our template and adjust the messages yourself based on your mind map and personal knowledge,** just…

1. Open a new Google doc and write out the example template we provided.

2. Copy and paste the same email 11 more times into this same document.

3. Look at your mind map and adjust the email templates one-by-one to speak to the different frustrations you know your customers have.

If you choose to use our template, combined with AI to generate your emails…

1. Copy the following prompt into your preferred AI tool (ChatGPT is the OG, so we usually recommend it):

2. *We're a B2B manufacturer of X. Our customers are frustrated by X. Write me an email that encourages the recipient to respond to me to talk about the solution to their frustration. The email should be no more than 175 words. Should contain a friendly greeting. Make a joke about working in X industry. And close with an open ended request to email me back, so the recipient is likely to respond directly to the email. I do not want this to sound salesy. Here is an example of the style I would like you to emulate with this email:* **here's where you paste in our email template.**

3. The AI will generate a version of the email you want, and you can adjust it as you like. The idea is to get good enough output from the AI that you can make 5 minutes of adjustments before it's ready to go to your audience.

Once the emails are written to your liking...

1. Open your email marketing platform and create a new email.
2. Choose the most basic template available (every platform has a simple, plain text email).
3. Paste your content into the template using the "paste as plain text" option when you right click. You don't want any formatting to carry over from your Google doc.
4. Check to make sure you selected or inputted your new, phantom email sender (we talked about this at the start of the chapter).
5. Schedule the email to send based on your schedule (which we also talked about at the start of this chapter).
6. You can now duplicate this email and input the text from your next plain text email into the duplicated template.
7. Rinse and repeat until your entire campaign is scheduled.

You and your colleagues will have to monitor the phantom inbox so you can respond in a timely way. That's part of the power of this type of campaign - responding as quickly as a human would.

You could even assign two junior staff members to monitor the inbox so you and your more experienced colleagues don't have to. Get those junior staff to inform you when an email comes in.

And having done all this, you are now nurturing new prospects attracted by your permission asset, existing contacts from previous purchases, and cold contacts who haven't worked with your business in a long time, at scale. **You're doing more than most teams at your largest competitors and positioning yourself for a good pay increase.**

How Conductors can make sure this gets done right

So much of your job is just keeping staff honest and giving them the tools to do well.

They feel like imposters because they don't know how to do everything, and they produce work that isn't up to your standard because they feel like imposters. Not because they aren't capable of the work, but because their fear shuts them down.

They're afraid of being found out.

But with the right guidance, you can nurture them so they can nurture your customers. So they stop performing like imposters and start shining like the skilled applicants you hired.

You can give your Creators the tools to do this right, so they have steps to follow and know exactly what you're looking for in their output.

And so you have the steps to review with them just as easily. You don't have to take mental time out of your day to review their work, you just have to go through the checklist with them and verify they've done it all.

And if their ideas aren't good (because contrary to the maxim, there definitely are bad ideas), you can help them improve those ideas easily.

First, how do you assign this nurturing campaign to your Creator?

Step 1. Buy them this book and get them to read chapter 13. Or send them the instructions at **www.jbbgi.com/resources** so they can read the section dedicated to them.

Step 2. Give them the mind map you created in chapter 4 of this book.

Step 3. Tell them you need this turned around by the end of the week (even if it's Friday, to make them sweat!).

Second, how do you evaluate the quality of their work?

There is a qualitative and a quantitative element to this.

To measure the quantitative element, review this checklist with them:

Does it contain space for dynamic text (for example, the lead's first name)?   ✓ | ✗

Does it contain fewer than 175 words?   ✓ | ✗

Does it contain an email signature from the phantom sender?   ✓ | ✗

Does it end with a question?   ✓ | ✗

Are the sentences and paragraphs broken up to avoid looking like a big wall of text?   ✓ | ✗

Does it talk about a frustration in your industry?   ✓ | ✗

Then, to measure the qualitative element.

Does it sound like the Creator knows what they're talking about?   ✓ | ✗

Does it contain platitudes (phrases that don't provide any value, like don't stop believin!)?   ✓ | ✗

Does it adequately describe the prospect's frustration?   ✓ | ✗

Is the closing question enticing (is it a small enough commitment to make the reader want to reach out)?   ✓ | ✗

When you read it, does it flow like a person speaking (that's the way we want it)?   ✓ | ✗

Does anything seem weird about it?   ✓ | ✗

The qualitative elements are where you can really start shaping Claire the Creator into an expert. A lead (and revenue) generating machine for your business.

If you answer in the negative to any of the qualitative questions, you can show your Creator exactly why.

This shows them you're investing your personal energy into their professional development, and it helps reduce the long-term burden of their learning on the business.

As you work through this checklist, you give them feedback they can write down and post all over their workspace. And they'll take it to heart the next time they perform this task for you.

Once these 12-24 emails are to your standard, Claire the Creator can build them out in your email marketing platform just as described in the Creator section of this chapter.

You can then require monthly reports on the results from this nurturing campaign to see how each individual email performs. And you can look at long term trends after about 8 months, to see if existing customers have increased spending with you. Sometimes the most important metrics aren't the clicks or opens of individual emails, but the long-term trends you can only start to see after some time has gone by.

And holy smokes Creators, Curators, Conductors. You've done it. You've completed all 6 steps of your lead-and-revenue-generating permission asset marketing and merchandising program.

Chapter 18

ENJOY THE FRUITS OF YOUR LABOR.

We want to close with a story to give you some confidence.

If you take one thing away from this book, other than the practical skills to do everything outlined in the last 17 chapters, it's that **you can thrive in any workplace.** You shouldn't feel like an imposter. Because you have those practical skills now, and that's more than most people in your role.

You can do all the things to make your business grow. Earn more money. Easily manage the people doing lead generation work for you.

We live in this world where people hide behind a veneer of expertise. We speak with authority about things we read a social media headline about. We're nervous to be learners - nervous to be found out as learners.

But it's alright not to be an expert yet. It's alright to learn new things forever. It's alright to be humble.

Because you don't need to be an expert in cement manufacturing to do amazing work for Lafarge. You don't need to know everything that goes on in every workflow in the lab to compete with the team generating leads for Thermo Fisher.

We wrote this book to help. Because there was a time when both of us had to overcome this imposter syndrome or be swallowed by it.

Back in the early 2000s, neither of us had experience in the B2B industry where we now spend the majority of our energies.

With no formal training in any of the sciences, just an interest and a platform, we both began writing magazine articles about science. This was at two different publishers in the same niche B2B industry, during the same stages of our careers. Because while it was daunting, it was also interesting. Exciting.

It was also slow. Everything took longer than it should have. Deadlines were missed. Stories bombed. Interviews bombed. Confidence was shattered.

What were the right angles? The right questions to ask? How much research was enough? When should that research happen? What research is trustworthy?

Endless questions. Long hours for low pay. Not sustainable.

Then we started building systems and following them fervently.

Not long after, we were both publishing cover stories for multiple trade publications in the laboratory and scientific research fields. The largest trade pubs in that market.

We're not saying we're special. No bragging here. In fact, the opposite. We're not special. We just built systems to help us work through things we didn't understand. So we could eventually understand well enough to write about it confidently to hundreds of thousands of readers. Readers that were PhDs and Physicists!

At this point in time, there was no such thing as content marketing. But when we paired up to transition our skills to generating sales leads for businesses, we realized creating content was the most powerful way to generate these leads. And we could supercharge that with the systems we'd developed to teach ourselves how to excel in the trade niches we were moving on from.

Running a business or generating leads for a business is the same as getting eyes on a magazine. You can't know everything. But you can use systems to get better, and build your understanding, and become one of the people others are intimidated by.

Everything from the start of this book until now is meant to move you toward a more rounded, nuanced understanding of the business you work in or run. The only way you get there is by accepting the things you don't know and searching for hopeful answers.

We actually wrote this book for 3 reasons we didn't talk about at the outset.

1. We wish we had confidence early in our careers and we want to help young people accelerate as fast as possible. So they can be happier at work, more fulfilled at home, and more certain of the direction they're taking.

2. We work with a lot of business owners and execs, and their largest pain point over the last 3 years has been staffing in marketing and sales leadership roles. This has a negative impact on company growth. A lot of the time, they have this problem because they can't compete with consumer brands for marketing talent. Or the new employee doesn't really know what they're getting into, and they leave quickly because they feel like imposters. Turnover is high, retention is low.

3. We're always disheartened to lose close connections - friends in the businesses we work with - when they leave to go work at a B2C company. We want these friendships to last. We want to see our friends thriving. We want our friends to get into a great flow in their industries so they can be the thought leaders in their own space.

We hope this book helps you.

Creators, a closing message for you.

We want you to be happy. We want you to be less stressed at work. We want you to look around at the sea of imposters and say *nope, not me*. We want you to earn more money.

Because you are us, and we wanted these things for ourselves. Doing your job confidently and well helps you achieve all this and more.

Don't worry about AI. AI can help you. Never replace you. Not if you look for deeper insights. Seek the hidden knowledge in your industry. AI can help prop you up.

Stand on its shoulders and see further.

Use this book to get the pay you want and the job you want. Don't chase a B2C job for the brand name. B2B is going to treat you better.

You're going to kill it, and we can't wait to hear about it.

Curators, we're so glad you took on this challenge.

Creating a permission asset and doing all the merchandising as a side-role in the business is no small ask.

When you follow the steps in this book, you're going to look like a hero.

You're going to achieve more than most dedicated marketing people, but you'll be less stressed than them.

And you're going to earn more money than them too. Because you're making yourself invaluable to the business.

By investing in this book you're investing in yourself. And you're taking control of your future. You can generate a torrent of leads that contribute directly to your success in your primary job role.

What most people talk about, you do. There are many things to be humble about, but this is not one of them. You're taking action where most people talk.

Hats off to you. We look forward to our next chat.

Conductors, thank you for your humility.

By investing in this book, you show you're exactly the person who should lead.

You're still learning, still looking for ways to be better, even though many in your position are content to cruise.

This is how you will get to live the life you want.

Trusting the people working under you improves your quality of life massively, alongside theirs. The systems in this book give them the power to do more excellent work independently. No more micromanaging. No more challenging evaluations.

There's a system. There are checklists. All they have to do is follow the plan. And all you have to do is verify they did it. After a few times, you won't even have to verify it. You'll be able to trust them entirely to run with it. Generate you leads. Revenue. And they'll love that trust.

Reward them with those salary increases. Because they're earning it. And because when they do better, you do much better.

We love talking to you. Reach out any time for a friendly chat about your growth, your weekend plans, your plans for the business next year - just email **friends@jbbgi.com**.

Congratulations. You've vanquished the imposter in you. You'll vanquish your competitors. And you didn't even break a sweat.

Thank you for taking this journey with us.

Appendix A:

SERVICES

If you're a B2B equipment manufacturer, distributor, or your firm provides services to other businesses, and you're **ready to increase your revenue**, here's how we can help:

1. The 6-Step B2B Sales Lead Journey you learned about in this book can be implemented quickly by our marketing and consulting agency, Journey Better Business Group Inc. Learn more at **www.jbbgi.com** or drop us an email to set up a Zoom chat. John Buie **john@jbbgi.com** or Jason Hagerman **jason@jbbgi.com**.

2. We've trained dozens of teams to get the ideas flowing and the workflow smooth. **If you want your team to implement the 6-Step Journey to its best effect, we're happy to help.** Once your staff is proficient in the Journey, they can implement it over and over again to grow your business, revenue, and profits.

3. Want to implement this Journey for other businesses, as an independent consultant, and **give yourself time, independence, and financial freedom**? We run a program for you to launch or grow your consulting or marketing agency business as a B2B Journey Certified Partner. You can learn more at **www.jbbgi.com/partner**.

4. If you require consulting for any aspect of growing your B2B business revenue, from product positioning to product development, from your tech stack to your payment flow, from conversion rate optimization to your manufacturer/distributor relationships, we're available on retainer.

Our services are delivered all over the world. We have as many clients in Japan and Germany as we do in the USA and Canada. And our monthly retainer for most services start at roughly the same price as one unpredictable and unproven new hire on your team. For that same investment of around $10k usd per month, you get a force multiplier on your entire team's efforts, that will drive revenue growth for your companies for the next decade.

5. Finally, we love speaking about the ideas in this book, and dozens of other tangents from these core ideas. If you have a podcast, webinar or live event you would like us to speak at, please get in touch.

Appendix B:

ACKNOWLEDGMENTS

Christopher S. Penn & John Wall
Drew McLellan
Dan Andrews & Ian Schoen
Bill Caskey & Bryan Neale
Mitch Joel
Dan Dayley
Michael Williams
Heinz Roesch
Jim Huggins
Brian McCutcheon
David C. Baker & Blair Enns
Pat Flynn
Gary Vaynerchuck
John Jantsch
Rand Fishkin
Craig Venter
Joanna Wiebe
Tim Stoddart
Chris Forbes
Dr. Wilf Keller